**COMMUNITY DEVELOPMENT
FINANCIAL INSTITUTIONS FUND**

Growth, Diversity, Impact:
A Snapshot of CDFIs in FY 2003

UNITED STATES DEPARTMENT OF THE TREASURY

WRITTEN BY

Donna Fabiani
Manager, Financial Strategies and Research

and

James Greer
Analyst, Financial Strategies and Research

The authors wish to thank the 223 CDFIs that contributed data for this report and the CIIS Help Desk staff for assisting the CDFIs and cleansing the data. This report could not have been written without their collective effort.

Message from the Director

June 1, 2007

I am pleased to release the first comprehensive analysis of annual Community Development Financial Institution (CDFI) performance data submitted to the CDFI Fund's Community Investment Impact System (CIIS). This report analyzes the FY 2003 performance data of 223 CDFIs, most of which are certified and funded by the CDFI Fund. I am also delighted to make the data set that this report is based on available to researchers, CDFIs, and other interested parties so that they may conduct further analysis on the disaggregated data.

In 2001, the Fund began collecting transaction level data from its awardees to measure their performance in much greater detail. In a partnership with systems developer EF Kearney Limited, the Fund spent two years designing and developing a system that could collect institution and transaction level data from Fund awardees.

CIIS was operational in June of 2004 when CDFIs and New Markets Tax Credit (NMTC) Program allocatees began reporting their FY 2003 activities. In the first year of reporting, CDFIs were required to submit institution level data, but not transaction level data. A small number of CDFIs did choose to submit transaction level data voluntarily. Throughout the fall of 2004 and winter of 2005, the Fund and EF Kearney worked with CDFIs and NMTC allocatees to complete and verify their first CIIS data submissions. In subsequent years we expect to significantly shorten the data collection and analysis process. The CDFI Fund looks forward to releasing additional reports in the future.

We hope this report will be a useful tool for those interested in understanding how CDFIs operate, the products and services they offer, and the impact they are making in the communities they serve.

Sincerely,

Kimberly A. Reed

Kimberly A. Reed
Director

Note: This page left blank intentionally.

Executive Summary

In June 2004, the Community Development Financial Institutions (CDFI) Fund launched the Community Investment Impact System (CIIS), a web-based data collection system that CDFI Fund awardees use to report their annual performance and compliance information to the Fund. In the summer and fall of 2004, 223 CDFIs submitted information on their fiscal year (FY) 2003 activities to the Fund via CIIS. This report presents the analysis of that data.

CIIS collects two types of information. The Institution Level Report covers the organization's financial activity and position, ownership characteristics, staffing levels and composition, technical assistance and training services, loan sales and loan purchases. The Transaction Level Report includes details on each loan or investment that a CDFI makes, including borrower and project addresses, borrower socio-economic characteristics, loan or investment terms, repayment status, and community development outcomes. For CDFIs that are not completing a Transaction Level Report, the Institution Level Report also covers financing activity, loan and investment portfolio outstanding, and community outcomes. At the time the data for this report was collected, CDFIs were not required to submit a Transaction Level Report, though six submitted the report voluntarily. The Transaction Level Report was a new reporting requirement that did not go into effect until CDFIs that received awards in FY 2003[1] began reporting for those awards (which in most cases was FY 2005). This report only analyzes data from 223 Institution Level Reports.

The 223 CIIS respondents are similar in institution type, geographic distribution, and age to the larger population of Fund-certified CDFIs. The CIIS respondents include 178 loan funds, 28 credit unions, nine venture funds, and eight banks.

The report analyzes data by type, age and size of CDFI. These breakouts demonstrate the differences between regulated and non-regulated institutions, and between lending organizations (loan funds) and equity investment organizations (venture funds).

The analysis shows that while many CDFIs have been providing financing for only a few years and most are relatively small financial institutions, on the whole they have provided *financial services*[2] in economically distressed areas and to individuals and others that lack access to credit, while maintaining an admirable level of financial health. The age and size analysis clearly shows that CDFIs are dynamic institutions that grow larger and financially stronger over time.

Following are the key findings from the report. These findings are for the 223 CDFIs as a whole.

- CDFIs have combined assets of $5.1 billion. Banks are by far the largest CDFIs, with average assets of $106 million. Loan funds follow with $22 million on average. Credit unions and venture funds each average $11 million in assets.

---

[1] The CDFI Fund's fiscal year 2003 began on October 1, 2002 and ended on September 30, 2003.
[2] Italicized terms are defined in the Glossary to this report.

■ CDFIs manage over $4 billion in lending and investing capital and have access to an additional $1 billion in off-balance sheet resources for lending and investing. Banks and other depository institutions provide nearly 25% of the $4 billion. Government provides less than 10%. The CDFI Fund provides less than 2%, a small but critical source because it is primarily difficult-to-find grant and equity capital which CDFIs can leverage to borrow additional capital.

■ CDFIs held a combined portfolio of loans and equity investments totaling over $3.4 billion at the end of FY 2003. Approximately 30% of the portfolio is in mortgage and home improvement loans; another 30% is in residential real estate construction and rehabilitation. When two large CDFI outliers[3] are excluded, the portfolio is more evenly distributed among sectors, with 25% in residential real estate development, 22% in business, 13% in mortgage and home improvement, and 13% in *commercial real estate* development.

■ CDFIs originated $1.7 billion in new loans and investments in FY 2003. When two large CDFI outliers are excluded, CDFIs originated $1.2 billion.

■ In FY 2003, CDFI financing helped to create or maintain nearly 8,000 jobs, develop or rehabilitate 40,000 housing units, and provide mortgage financing to more than 3,000 first-time homeowners. CDFIs provided development services (i.e., technical assistance and training to borrowers or potential borrowers) to more than 50,000 people and organizations. CDFIs managed nearly 39,000 *Individual Development Accounts* (IDAs) with a combined savings balance of $2 million.

■ A small number of CDFIs were active in the *secondary market*. Twenty-six CDFIs sold 4,900 loans with a total presale book value of $524 million. Most loan sales were at par. An even smaller number of CDFIs —18 — purchased loans of more than $1 billion.

■ Self-sufficiency rates (the extent to which a CDFI is covering its operating expenses through earned income rather than through grants or other contributions) grew from an average of 40% for the youngest CDFIs to 79% for the oldest CDFI.

■ Three-year average net revenue was positive and increasing for all CDFI age and size groups.

■ The average loan loss rate per CDFI was 2.2% and the average portfolio at risk rate per CDFI was 4.4%. The loan loss rate for the combined portfolio of all CIIS respondents was less than one percent (.7%) in FY 2003 and the portfolio at risk was 2.5%.[4]

The above findings are described in detail in the body of the report. Where appropriate, they are provided by type, age and size of CDFI.

---

[3] Outliers are data that are either significantly larger or smaller than the rest of the data in a sample. Outliers skew the analysis by inflating or deflating the average and are therefore typically removed from the analysis.

[4] For a detailed explanation of the difference between the average and combined portfolio rates, see Chapter IX. When comparin loan loss and portfolio at risk rates to the CDFI Data Project (CDP) analysis, the combined portfolio rates should be used.

Table of Contents

Note: This page left blank intentionally.

I. Introduction

 ## Introduction to this Report

In June 2004, the Community Development Financial Institutions (CDFI) Fund launched the Community Investment Impact System (CIIS), a web-based data collection system that CDFIs use to report their annual performance information to the Fund. In the summer of 2004, 223 CDFI Program awardees, Native Initiatives awardees, and non-awardee certified CDFIs submitted information on their fiscal year (FY) 2003 activities to the Fund via CIIS. This report analyzes the data provided by those 223 CDFIs.[1]

Chapters II and III of this report compare the population of all Fund-certified CDFIs to the sample of CDFIs that submitted CIIS data. Chapters IV through X analyze CDFIs' FY 2003 performance.

A copy of the CIIS data collection instrument is found in Appendix A. A description of the Fund's data collection and analysis methodologies is found in Appendix B. Appendix C provides an explanation of statistical terms used in this report. Definitions of italicized terms are found in the glossary in Appendix D.

As some readers are aware, a similar data collection and analysis was conducted by the CDFI Data Project (CDP) on the FY 2003 activities of 477 institutions. (See "Providing Capital, Building Communities, Creating Impact: Community Development Financial Institutions, FY 2003," Third Edition, a publication of the CDFI Data Project.) While the performance of institutions in the CDP sample is generally comparable to the performance of CDFIs in the CIIS sample, there are several differences in the institutions analyzed. There are also some discrepancies in responses provided by institutions that responded to both CIIS and the CDP. For a comparison of the samples and key results, see Appendix E. Appendix F includes additional portfolio quality analysis that can be used to compare the portfolio quality of the CIIS and CDP respondents.

 ## Introduction to the CDFI Fund

The CDFI Fund was created for the purpose of promoting economic revitalization and community development through investment in and assistance to CDFIs. The Fund was established through the Reigle Community Development and Regulatory Improvement Act of 1994, as a bipartisan initiative. The Fund also manages the New Markets Tax Credit (NMTC) Program, which was authorized by the Community Renewal Tax Relief Act of 2000.

The Fund achieves its purpose by promoting access to capital and local economic growth in the following ways: 1) through its CDFI Program by directly investing in, supporting and training CDFIs that provide

---

[1] While the 223 CIIS respondents are similar to the universe of more than 700 certified CDFIs, differences in the two groups do exist. Therefore, one cannot conclude that the findings in this report apply to all certified CDFIs.

loans, investments, financial services and technical assistance to underserved populations and communities; 2) through its New Markets Tax Credit (NMTC) Program by providing an allocation of tax credits to community development entities (CDEs) which enable them to attract investment from the private-sector and reinvest these amounts in Low-Income Communities; 3) through its Bank Enterprise Award (BEA) Program by providing an incentive to banks to invest in their communities and in CDFIs; and 4) through its Native Initiatives by providing financial assistance, technical assistance, and training to Native CDFIs and other Native entities proposing to become or create Native CDFIs.

Since its creation through FY 2006, the CDFI Fund has awarded $820 million to community development organizations and financial institutions; it has awarded allocations of New Markets Tax Credits which will attract private-sector investments totaling $12.1 billion, including $600 million for the Gulf Opportunity Zone.

Additional information on the CDFI Fund and its programs is available on the CDFI Fund's website at: www.cdfifund.gov.

Comparison of CIIS Respondents and All Certified CDFIs

To fully appreciate the findings presented in this report, one must understand what a CDFI is and have some knowledge of the universe of certified CDFIs. This chapter provides that background. As well, it introduces the sample of 223 CDFIs that are analyzed in the report.

The Fund defines a CDFI as an organization that meets six criteria.

The organization:

1. Has a primary mission of promoting community development;

2. Is a *Financing Entity*;

3. Principally serves an economically distressed area, low-income population, or other population that lacks access to financing (known as an eligible *Target Market*);

4. Provides technical assistance, training or other *Development Services* in conjunction with its financing activities;

5. Is accountable to its *Target Market* through representation on its board or other means; and

6. Is a non-governmental entity that is not controlled by one or more governmental entities.

An organization that meets all six criteria can be certified as a CDFI by the Fund. As of the end of FY 2003, the Fund had certified 723 CDFIs.[1] Certified CDFIs include loan funds[2], credit unions, community development banks, and community development venture capital funds, among others.

It should be noted that while organizations must meet the Fund's criteria to become certified CDFIs, not all organizations that meet these criteria apply for certification. By some estimates, there are approximately 1,000 institutions in the United States that meet a broader definition of a CDFI as being a "specialized financial institution whose core purpose is to provide financial products and services to people and communities underserved by traditional financial markets."[3]

---

[1] The number of certified CDFIs had grown to 773 by December 31, 2006. For purposes of this report, analysis and comparisons are based on the 723 organizations that were certified as of September 30, 2003, the end of the Fund's FY 2003.

[2] The Fund classifies community development corporations (CDCs), including bank CDCs, as loan funds.

[3] "Providing Capital, Building Communities, Creating Impact: CDFIs," The CDFI Data Project's FY 2003 report.

**There are many types
of certified CDFIs.**

As Figure 2-1 shows, regulated financial institutions
(primarily credit unions and to a much smaller
extent, banks) represent more than one-quarter
(26%) of all certified CDFIs. Loan funds, which
are typically non-profit organizations specializing
in business, microenterprise, housing and/or
community facilities financing, represent nearly
all of the remaining three-quarters. Community
development venture capital funds represent a
very small proportion of all CDFIs (4%).

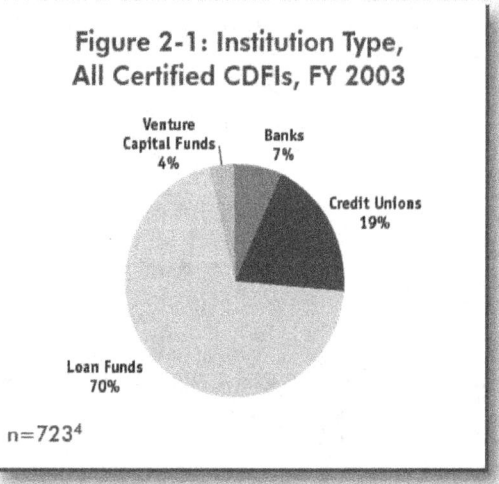

**Figure 2-1: Institution Type,
All Certified CDFIs, FY 2003**

n=723[4]

 Certified CDFIs are located in all areas of the country.

Figure 2-2 shows the location, by headquarters, of all certified CDFIs in the United States. Certified CDFIs
are located in every state as well as the District of Columbia, Puerto Rico, and the U.S. Virgin Islands.
CDFIs are located in both urban and rural areas, in communities that are predominantly minority and
those predominantly non-minority, and in communities with widely varying economic challenges and
opportunities. There are concentrations of CDFIs in the mid-Atlantic and the Northeast, throughout
Appalachia, the upper Mississippi Delta, and the major metropolitan areas of the west coast.

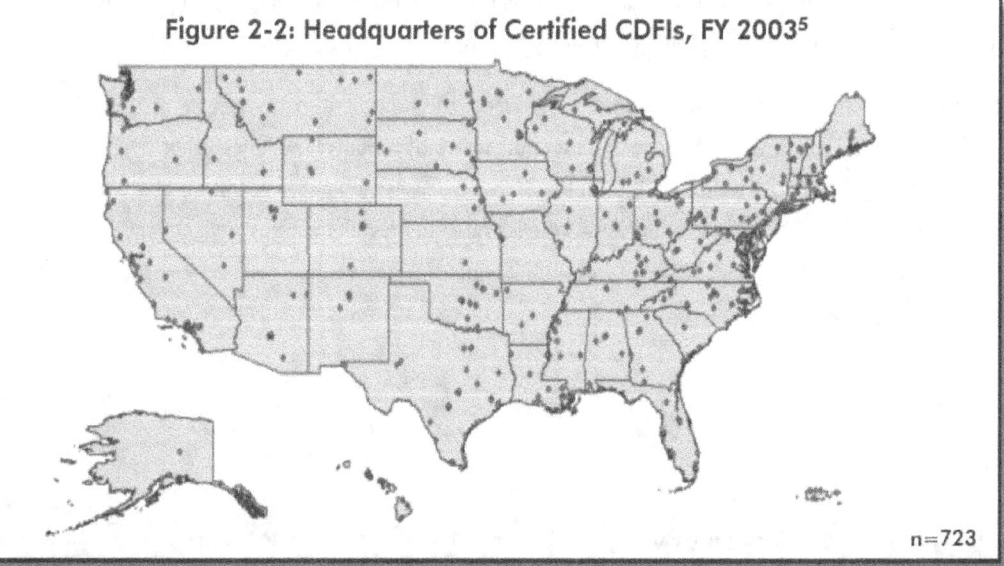

Figure 2-2: Headquarters of Certified CDFIs, FY 2003[5]

n=723

---

[4] "n" refers to the number of certified CDFIs represented in the figure.

[5] The U.S. Virgin Islands are not shown. There is one certified CDFI headquartered in the U.S. Virgin Islands.

 A subset of certified CDFIs is analyzed in this report.

As of the introduction of CIIS in 2004, entities that receive monetary awards through the Fund's CDFI Program and Native Initiatives are required to submit CIIS reports annually during the term of their assistance agreements with the Fund. Of the 223 FY 2003 CIIS respondents, 214 are certified CDFIs. The nine respondents that are not certified CDFIs are Fund awardees that expected to become certified CDFIs within two years of receiving their Fund awards.

 CIIS respondents are similar to, though not always statistically representative of, all certified CDFIs.

As shown in Figure 2-3, the 223 CIIS respondents are similar in institution type to the population of all certified CDFIs. For both CIIS respondents and all certified CDFIs, loan funds represent the largest group followed by credit unions, which represent a substantial share. In both groups, banks and venture funds represent a small share of all CDFIs. In terms of numbers of CIIS respondents, there are 178 loan funds, 28 credit unions, nine venture funds, and eight banks.

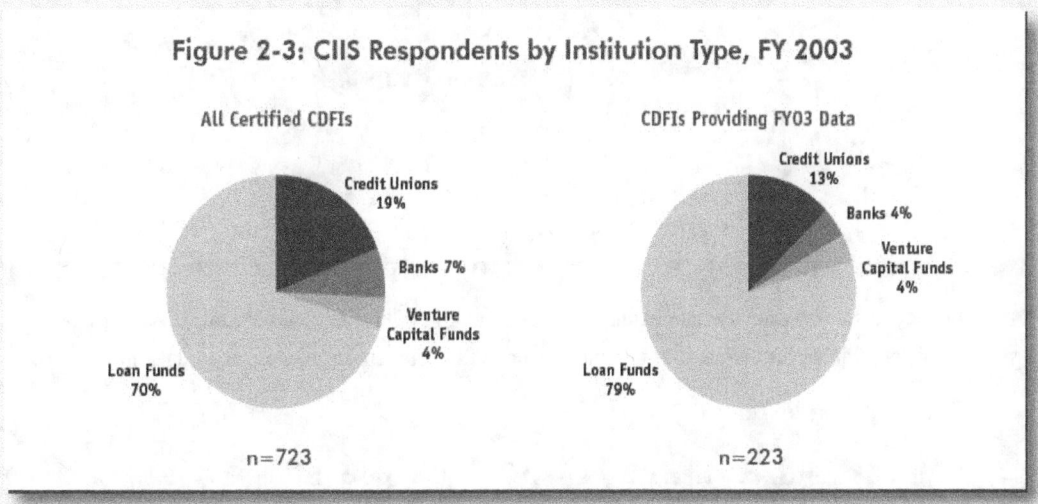

Figure 2-3: CIIS Respondents by Institution Type, FY 2003

There are differences between the 223 CIIS respondents and all certified CDFIs that should be noted. First, loan funds are a larger share of CIIS respondents (79% versus 70%). Second, credit unions and banks are a smaller proportion of CIIS respondents than of all certified CDFIs. While 13% of CIIS respondents are credit unions, nearly one-fifth (19%) of all certified CDFIs are credit unions. The same is true for banks. Banks represent 4% of CIIS respondents but nearly double that proportion (7%) of all certified CDFIs. The proportion of venture funds among CIIS respondents and all certified CDFIs is identical (4%).

Like all certified CDFIs, CIIS respondents are distributed widely throughout the country, with a concentration in the northeast. See Figure 2-4. However, a state by state comparison of certified CDFIs and CIIS respondents shows that there is a statistically significant difference between the proportion of certified CDFIs headquartered in each state and the proportion of CIIS respondents headquartered in each state (t=7.66 p < .001)[6]. And while certified CDFIs exist in every state, careful examination of Figure 2-4 reveals that there are two states from which no CDFI provided data for this report—North Dakota and Michigan.[7]

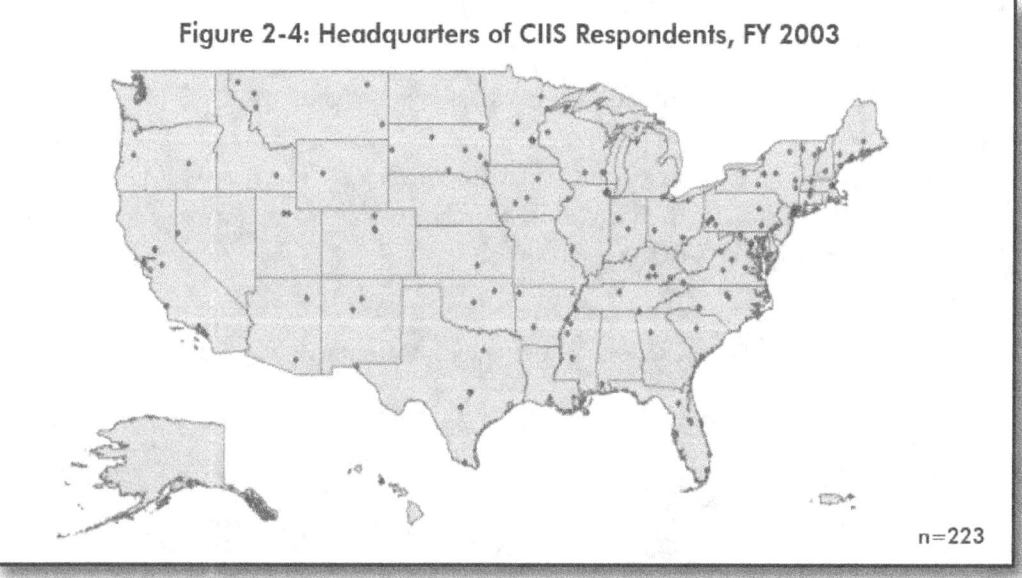

Figure 2-4: Headquarters of CIIS Respondents, FY 2003

n=223

In terms of age as measured by the number of years since the CDFI was incorporated, there is no statistically significant difference between all certified CDFIs and those that provided data in FY 2003 (F=.785 p<.376).

 CIIS respondents are very similar to the pool of CDFI Program and Native Initiatives awardees.

Not surprisingly, the CIIS respondents are closely representative of the pool of CDFI Program and Native Initiatives awardees. Figure 2-5 shows the proportion of CDFI Program and Native Initiatives awardees by financial institution type. Comparing this figure to Figure 2-3 reveals the similarity between the share of awards by institution type and the institutional composition of CIIS respondents. A few examples should

---

[6] See Appendix C for an explanation of statistical terms used in this report.

[7] While CDFIs in Michigan and North Dakota have received CDFI Program awards, no North Dakota CDFIs were required to report on their FY 2003 performance and the data from the Michigan CDFIs required to report were not included due to technical problems with their data submissions.

suffice here. Loan funds represent 79% of both the awardees and the CIIS respondents. Credit unions represent 15% of awardees and 13% of the CIIS respondents. Banks and venture funds received 2% and 3% respectively of the Fund's awards, and each represent 4% of the CIIS respondents. Figure 2-5 shows that one percent of the awardees are not financial institutions. These organizations are sponsoring entities (Native organizations, tribes, and tribal organizations) that propose to create Native CDFIs under the Native Initiatives Program.

In terms of award type, Native Initiatives awardees are under-represented among the CIIS respondents. Native CDFIs and tribal sponsors of emerging CDFIs represent 11% of awardees during the noted period. Of the 223 total organizations providing data for this report, 10 (5%) were Native CDFIs or emerging Native CDFIs and one (<0.1%) was a sponsor of an emerging CDFI. These results are not surprising because sponsoring entities were not required to provide data to CIIS. The one sponsoring entity noted in this report is also a certified CDFI and awardee of a CDFI program award.

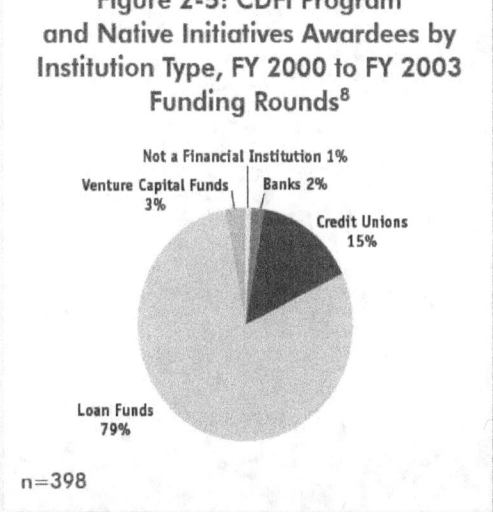

Figure 2-5: CDFI Program and Native Initiatives Awardees by Institution Type, FY 2000 to FY 2003 Funding Rounds[8]

Not a Financial Institution 1%
Venture Capital Funds 3%
Banks 2%
Credit Unions 15%
Loan Funds 79%
n=398

This chapter has provided a broad comparison of the 223 CIIS respondents and all certified CDFIs and has shown that while the two groups are similar, statistically significant differences do exist. Given these differences, the reader should refrain from concluding that the findings in this report apply to all certified CDFIs.

---

[8]The period FY 2000 through FY 2003 was selected because these are the years for which the awards data was most readily available.

Note: This page left blank intentionally.

III. Characteristics of CIIS Respondents

The previous chapter compared the institution type and headquarters location of certified CDFIs with the same information for the 223 CIIS respondents. This chapter examines the characteristics of the CIIS respondents in more detail. Unless otherwise noted, throughout this report the term "CDFIs" refers to the 223 CIIS respondents.

This chapter continues to analyze CDFIs by financial institution type, demonstrating the wide range of differences among types. One important distinction is the regulated versus non-regulated status of CDFIs. Credit unions and banks are depository institutions that operate in a highly regulated environment. Their financial policies and practices must comply with guidance issued by their respective regulators. In contrast, loan funds and venture funds are non-depository, non-regulated institutions. There is no oversight body that dictates their policies and procedures. Within the non-regulated institutions, there are other important differences. Venture funds provide equity and equity-like products to for-profit businesses while loan funds tend to offer debt and sometimes equity products to a wide range of clients including individuals, for-profit businesses, and non-profit businesses. As will be seen below, institution types vary widely across a range of characteristics, including age, size, tax status and type of ownership.

 CDFIs are young relative to traditional financial institutions.

CDFIs in the sample have been providing financing for 14 years on average, with a median of 10 years. By comparison, the average age of all regulated credit unions, including thousands of credit unions that are not certified CDFIs, is 48 years, with a median of 49 years.[1]

Within the group of CIIS respondents, bank and credit union CDFIs are significantly older than both loan funds and venture funds. See Figure 3-1. However, credit union CDFIs are younger than all credit unions, with an average age of 28 years and a median of 23 years. Age of CDFI, by type, is similar across regions in the U.S.

[1] Source: National Federation of Community Development Credit Unions.

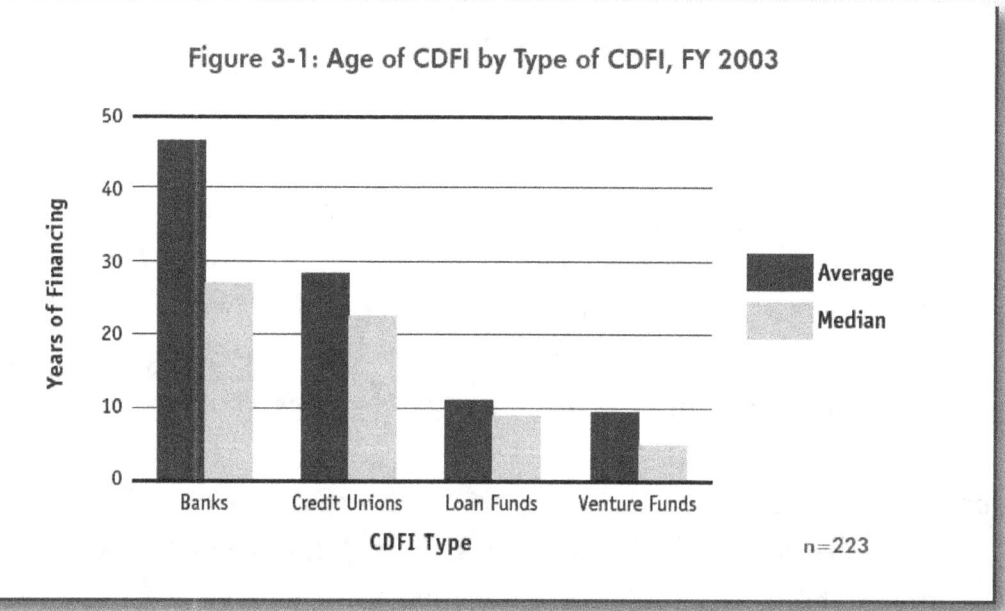

Figure 3-1: Age of CDFI by Type of CDFI, FY 2003

 CDFIs are modestly sized financial institutions.

The CIIS respondents are relatively small financial institutions when compared to traditional financial institutions. The 223 CIIS respondents have combined assets of more than $5.1 billion, with average assets of $23.1 million and median assets of $5.1 million. By comparison with the traditional financial sector, the average assets of all regulated credit unions was $71.9 million and for all commercial banks $1.1 billion.[2] Table 3-1 shows the total, average, and median assets of CIIS respondents by type of CDFI. The table includes a row for loan funds excluding three loan funds that have very large assets in comparison to most of the loan funds analyzed in this study. These three loan funds are, in statistical terms, "outliers" that inflate the average. When the values of the outliers are removed, the resulting average is significantly lower.[3]

---

[2] Source: Federal Deposit Insurance Corporation (FDIC) at www3.fdic.gov/sdi for bank data. The National Federation for Community Development Credit Unions (NFCDCU) provided credit union data files. See also National Credit Union Administration (NCUA) at www.ncua.gov for additional data on credit unions.

[3] Throughout this report, outliers are identified and in most cases removed from the analysis. For more information on outliers, see Appendix C. Explanation of Statistical Terms Used in this Report.

Table 3-1: Assets by Type of CDFI, FY 2003

	n	Mean	Median	All CDFIs
Banks	8	$106,375,500	$109,100,500	$851,004,000
Credit Unions	28	$11,014,541	$5,731,833	$308,407,157
Loan Funds	178	$21,903,141	$4,392,746	$3,898,759,040
Loan Funds Less Outliers	*175*	*$11,171,036*	*$4,344,040*	*$1,954,931,259*
Venture Funds	9	$10,987,924	$3,415,007	$98,891,314
Total	223	$23,125,836	$5,118,687	$5,157,061,511

Table 3-1 shows that while the average CDFI bank has only one-tenth of the $1 billion in assets of traditional commercial banks, it has much greater assets than other types of CDFIs[4]. The average assets of CDFI banks are $106 million, or nearly four times the overall average of $23 million. Other types of CDFIs have more comparable, and moderate, asset levels. Average assets for credit unions, venture funds, and loan funds (disregarding loan fund outliers) are nearly identical at about $11 million. The median asset level for loan funds, credit unions, and venture funds, probably a more accurate gauge of the assets of these CDFIs, demonstrates graphically just how small most CDFIs are: the median assets for credit unions is $6 million, for loan funds $4 million, and for venture funds $3 million.

The information in the last column of this table reveals the overall importance of unregulated loan funds to the 223 respondents. While individual loan funds are on average relatively small institutions, the 178 loan funds in the sample control 76% of assets, nearly $4 billion. CDFI banks had over $851 million in assets, or about 17% of all CDFI assets. Credit unions controlled just over $300 million in assets, and venture funds nearly $100 million.

---

[4] CDFI banks are large relative to other CDFIs because like all regulated banks, they must meet certain minimum capital requirements set by their regulators.

THE LOAN FUND OUTLIERS

Center for Community Self-Help (Self-Help): The mission of the non-profit Self-Help and its financing affiliates, Self-Help Credit Union and Self-Help Ventures Fund, is to create ownership and economic opportunities for minorities, women, rural residents, and low-wealth families. Since 1980, Self-Help has provided $4.5 billion in financing to over 50,000 small businesses, nonprofits, and homebuyers. In addition to providing both conforming and non-conforming mortgage loans to individuals and families, Self-Help is expanding the pool of funds available to low-wealth homebuyers around the country by developing a *secondary market* for non-conforming home loans. Under the program, Self-Help purchases these home loans from lending institutions around the country. The participating lenders are required to use the liquidity gained through this program to make new loans to low-wealth families. Fannie Mae is committed to purchase the home loans that Self-Help acquires. Self-Help operates from seven regional offices in North Carolina, as well as an office in Washington, D.C. Self-Help had total assets of $1.1 billion as of the end of its fiscal year 2003.

Community Preservation Corporation (CPC): Headquartered in New York City, CPC is a private mortgage lender specializing in financing low-, moderate- and middle-income housing throughout New York and New Jersey. CPC has been involved in the financing of the refurbishing of multi-family dwellings as well as the conversion of previously commercial space into affordable multi-family dwellings. Sponsored by 94 banks and insurance companies, CPC has, since 1974, financed more than 117,000 *affordable housing* units, representing an investment of more than $5.3 billion. CPC's mission is to stabilize, strengthen, and sustain low- and mixed-income communities. CPC has branch offices throughout New York City as well as other major urban centers in the states of New York and New Jersey. CPC had total assets of $679 million as of the end of its fiscal year 2003.

Local Initiatives Support Corporation (LISC): A nation-wide organization dedicated to supporting community based development organizations, LISC provides capital, technical expertise, and training to resident-led groups. Since 1980, LISC has supported over 2,800 nonprofits with over $6 billion in grants, loans, and equity. Through these and other investments, LISC has created over 161,000 homes and apartments, 25 million square feet of commercial and community space, and 60,000 new jobs. LISC has branch offices in urban centers throughout the country. LISC had total assets of $327 million as of the end of its fiscal year 2003.

 CDFI staffing levels range from an average of four for venture funds to 40 for banks.

The number of employees of CDFIs is also relatively small. For the purposes of this analysis, consultants that perform ongoing operations are included when counting *full-time equivalent (FTE)* employees. Including consultants, the total number of *FTEs* of the 223 CDFIs providing data was 3,269, or an average of 15 *FTEs* per CDFI. In contrast, the average number of *FTEs* for credit unions in the U.S. was 24, for commercial banks the comparable figure was 237 *FTEs*, and for savings banks the comparable figure was 207 *FTEs*.

Figure 3-2 shows the average and median number of *FTEs* by type of CDFI in FY 2003. Banks clearly have a much larger number of *FTEs*, averaging 40 *FTE* compared to 15 *FTEs* for loan funds, 10 for credit unions, and four for venture funds. The median number of *FTEs* should also be noted. With the exception of the banks and venture funds, the median number of *FTEs* is much smaller than the mean. These median *FTE* figures also show that loan funds and credit unions are comparably sized with the median number of *FTEs* being six. Venture funds have just three median *FTEs*.

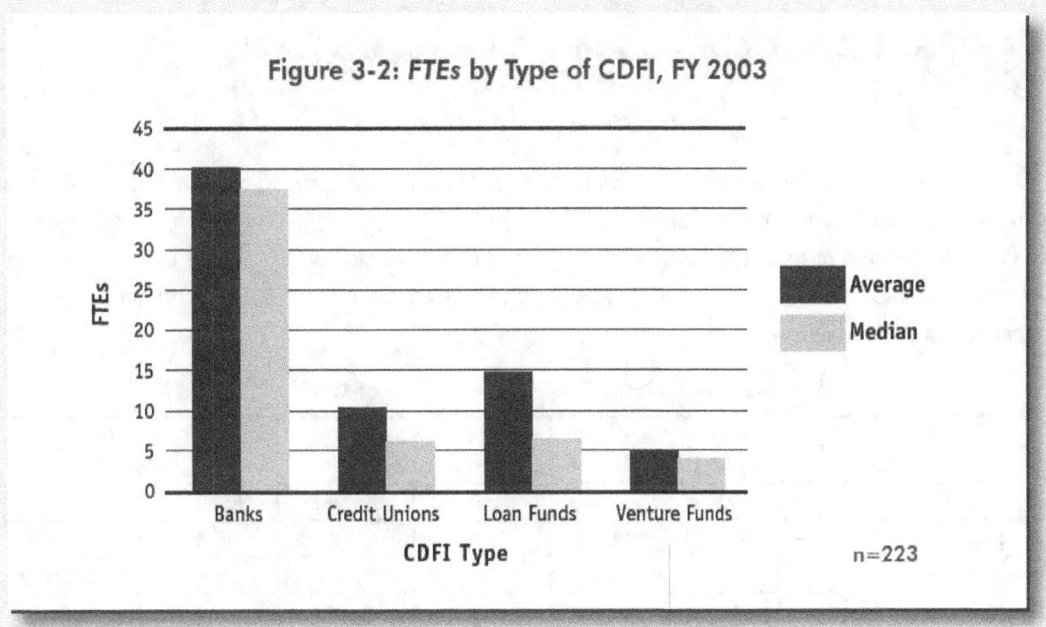

Figure 3-2: *FTEs* by Type of CDFI, FY 2003

▶ Most CDFIs are non-profit institutions.

CDFIs are primarily non-profit institutions. As summarized in Table 3-2, only 8.1% of CIIS respondents are for-profit institutions. Like all banks nationally, all CDFI banks are organized as for-profit firms. In contrast, all credit unions in the sample and nationally are non-profit institutions. The community development venture funds in the sample are nearly evenly split between for-profit and non-profit firms. In contrast, traditional venture capital funds in the U.S. are primarily organized as for-profit. A far majority of loan funds are organized as non-profit institutions.

Table 3-2: Tax Status of CDFIs by Type of CDFI, FY 2003

	For-Profit CDFIs		Non-Profit CDFIs	
	Number	Percent	Number	Percent
Banks	8	100.0%	0	0.0%
Credit Unions	0	0.0%	28	100.0%
Loan Funds	6	3.4%	172	96.6%
Venture Funds	4	44.4%	5	55.6%
Total	18	8.1%	205	91.9%

▶ Nearly 25% of CDFIs are *minority owned or controlled;* a smaller number are *women owned or controlled,* and *faith-based organizations.*

At least one-fifth of each type of CDFI is **minority owned or controlled**. Among regulated institutions the percentages are higher: more than one-third (37.5%) of banks and nearly half (46.4%) of credit unions are minority owned or controlled. Smaller percentages of non-regulated CDFIs and credit unions are *women owned or controlled*. A small number of credit unions and loan funds are *faith-based institutions*. These data are shown in Table 3-3.

Table 3-3: Ownership of CDFIs by Type of CDFI, FY 2003

	Minority Owned or Controlled CDFIs		Women Owned or Controlled CDFIs		Faith-Based CDFIs	
	Number	Percent	Number	Percent	Number	Percent
Banks	3	37.5%	0	0.0%	0	0.0%
Credit Unions	13	46.4%	4	14.3%	4	14.3%
Loan Funds	36	20.2%	30	16.9%	10	5.6%
Venture Funds	2	22.2%	2	22.2%	0	0.0%
Total	54	24.2%	36	16.2%	14	6.3%

n=223

 CDFIs serve many minority populations.

CDFIs provide services to many minority populations throughout the country. This is summarized in Table 3-4. Nearly three-quarters (73.6%) of the CDFIs reported that they provided services to Blacks or African Americans, almost two-thirds (61.7%) reported that they provided services to Hispanics or Latinos, nearly half (43.4%) reported providing services to Asians and a quarter (23.8%) of CDFIs reported providing services to Native Americans.

Table 3-4: CDFIs Serving Specific Racial/Ethnic Populations, FY 2003

	CDFIs Responding[5]	CDFIs Responding "Yes"	Percent Responding "Yes"
Alaska Native	186	4	2.2%
Asian	196	85	43.4%
Black or African American	208	153	73.6%
Hispanic or Latino	201	124	61.7%
Native American	185	44	23.8%
Native Hawaiian	182	6	3.3%
Other Pacific Islander	179	17	9.5%
White	211	179	84.8%
Other	179	92	51.4%

 CDFIs serve *faith-based organizations*.

Over a quarter (25.6%) of all CDFIs reported that they had provided financing to *faith-based organizations*. As Table 3-5 shows, a large percentage of banks and credit unions provided financing to *faith-based organizations*; a smaller percentage of loan funds did likewise.

Table 3-5: Financing Faith-Based Organizations by Type of CDFI, FY 2003

	CDFIs Responding	CDFIs Responding "Yes"	Percent Responding "Yes"
Banks	8	7	87.5%
Credit Unions	28	16	57.1%
Loan Funds	178	34	19.1%
Venture Funds	9	0	0.0%
Total	223	57	25.6%

[5] The number of CDFIs responding equals the number of CDFIs that responded "yes" or "no" to this question. CDFIs that answered "don't know" are excluded.

▶ CDFIs serve both urban and rural communities, including areas of persistent poverty.

A majority (60.5%) of CDFIs provided financial services to rural areas and an almost comparable proportion (52.7%) reported providing services to *major urban areas*, defined as Metropolitan Statistical Areas (MSAs) with populations of one million or more. A majority (59.2%) of CDFIs reported that they provide services in *minor urban areas*, defined as MSAs with populations of less than one million. These data are shown in Table 3-6.

A number of CDFIs report that they provide services to four areas of the country that are known for their persistent poverty. All of these areas are rural or primarily rural. As shown in Table 3-6, 11.5% of CDFIs report that they serve *Native American areas* and 10.6% report that they serve *Appalachia*. Smaller numbers of CDFIs report that they serve the *Colonias* along the U.S. – Mexico border (4.6%) as well as the *Lower Mississippi Delta* (4.1%).

Business owner Eva Gilbert is a client and business training graduate of Four Bands Community Fund, a CDFI located in Eagle Butte, South Dakota that serves the Cheyenne River Indian Reservation.

SOURCE: Four Bands Community Fund

Table 3-6: CDFIs Serving Specific Geographies, FY 2003

	CDFIs Responding[6]	CDFIS Responding "Yes"	Percent Responding "Yes"
URBAN/RURAL AREAS			
Major Urban Area	220	116	52.7%
Minor Urban Area	218	129	59.2%
Rural Areas	220	133	60.5%
AREAS OF PERSISTENT POVERTY			
Appalachia	218	23	10.6%
Colonias	218	10	4.6%
Lower Mississippi Delta	221	9	4.1%
Native American Areas	217	25	11.5%

[6] The number of CDFIs responding equals the number of CDFIs that responded "yes" or "no" to this question. CDFIs that answered "don't know" are excluded.

 Rural and urban CDFIs are significantly different.

As described above, CDFIs serve both urban and rural areas. Since CDFIs can serve large and diverse communities, a single CDFI may serve both urban and rural areas. Nearly one-fifth (17.9%) of CDFIs reported financing solely in rural areas and twice that (35.9%) reported financing only in urban areas.[7] The differences between these two groups are striking, as demonstrated in Table 3-7.

A higher proportion of rural CDFIs are banks (7.5%) and venture funds (5.0%), compared to urban CDFIs (3.8% banks and 2.5% venture funds). Rural CDFIs are older and larger than their urban counterparts. The average number of years a rural CDFI has been providing financing is 23 compared to 12 for urban CDFIs. Average total assets for rural CDFIs are $17.2 million compared to $13.8 million for urban CDFIs. While minority ownership is significant (22.5%) among rural CDFIs, women-owned or controlled CDFIs are few (2.5%) and faith-based CDFIs are non-existent among rural CDFIs. Urban CDFIs have more diverse ownership characteristics: one-third (33.8%) are minority owned or controlled, one-fifth (20.3%) are *women owned or controlled*, and 7.5% are *faith-based organizations*. Finally, a significantly larger percentage of urban CDFIs serve each minority population, with the exception of Native Americans, which rural CDFIs are more than twice as likely to serve.

Table 3-7: Characteristics of Rural and Urban CDFIs, FY 2003

	Serve Rural Only	Serve Urban Only
n	40	80
INSTITUTION TYPE		
Banks	7.5%	3.8%
Credit Unions	15.0%	15.0%
Loan Funds	72.5%	78.8%
Venture Funds	5.0%	2.5%
Total	100.0%	100.0%
AGE AND SIZE		
Average Years Financing	23	12
Average Total Assets	$17,168,066	$13,833,991
Average FTEs	11	12
OWNERSHIP AND CONTROL		
Minority Owned or Controlled	22.5%	33.8%
Women Owned or Controlled	2.5%	20.3%
Faith-Based Organization	0.0%	7.5%
POPULATIONS SERVED (% of CDFIs serving the populations)		
Asian	15.4%	56.2%
Black or African American	41.0%	93.5%
Hispanic or Latino	32.4%	73.3%
Native American	31.6%	16.4%
White	80.0%	88.3%

[7] None of the outliers serve only rural or only urban areas.

 Age and size peer group analysis

Much of the analysis in the remainder of this report will be based on age and size peer groupings of CDFIs. Age is defined as the number of years the CDFI has been financing. Size is determined by assets.

There is considerable variance in both of these variables. For instance, the number of years of financing ranged from one to 120, with an average of 14 and a median of 10. The range of assets was also quite large. Three CDFIs reported having assets of $24,000 or less in FY 2003, while the largest CDFI reported assets exceeding $937 million.

For the age and size peer group analysis, CDFIs are split into four groups of roughly equal numbers of CDFIs.

AGE: YEARS OF FINANCING

- Four years or less (59 CDFIs)

- Five to less than 10 years (50 CDFIs)

- 10 to less than 18 years (55 CDFIs)

- 18 years or more (59 CDFIs)

SIZE: TOTAL ASSETS

- Less than $1.5 million in assets (52 CDFIs)

- $1.5 million to less than $5 million in assets (58 CDFIs)

- $5 million to less than $15 million in assets (54 CDFIs)

- $15 million or more in assets (59 CDFIs)

The method used to divide CDFIs into these groups is straightforward. CDFIs were sorted and ranked by age and by size of total assets. These rankings were examined to identify any "natural breaks" in the data. CDFIs were then separated into groups of more or less the same size. Because the distributions of CDFIs had a tendency to bunch at certain points (this was especially true for the age of CDFI), it was not possible to split CDFIs into groups of exactly the same size.

 Characteristics of CDFIs by age

Looking first at age, Figure 3-3 and Table 3-8 show breakdowns by type of CDFI for each of the four age groups. These groups are fairly similar in terms of the composition of institution types. In each age group, all types of CDFIs are found and loan funds represent the largest share. Regulated CDFIs — banks and credit unions — and venture funds are found as a small proportion of each group except the oldest

group where credit unions make up 32.2% of the CDFIs. This is the only noticeable difference between all of the age groups.

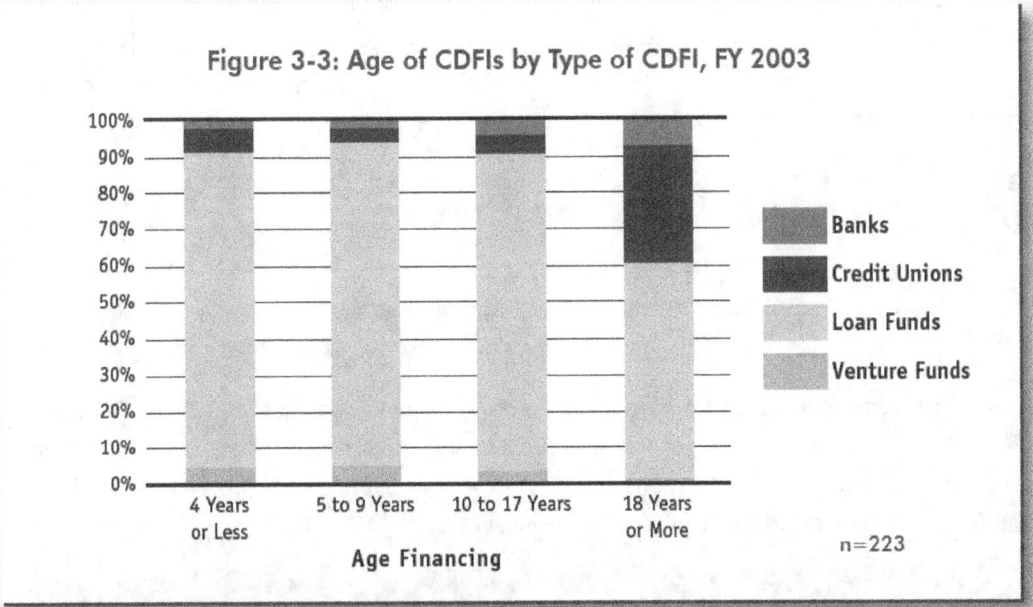

Figure 3-3: Age of CDFIs by Type of CDFI, FY 2003

n=223

Table 3-8: Age of CDFIs by Type of CDFI, FY 2003

	4 Years or Less		5 to 9 Years		10 to 17 Years		18 Years or More		All CDFIs	
Banks	1	1.7%	1	2.0%	2	3.6%	4	6.8%	8	3.6%
Credit Unions	4	6.8%	2	4.0%	3	5.5%	19	32.2%	28	12.6%
Loan Funds	51	86.4%	44	88.0%	48	87.3%	35	59.3%	178	79.8%
Venture Funds	3	5.1%	3	6.0%	2	3.6%	1	1.7%	9	4%
Total	59	100%	50	100%	55	100%	59	100%	223	100%

 Ownership of younger CDFIs is more diverse.

Table 3-9 shows the percentage of CDFIs in each age group that is owned or controlled by minorities or women as well as the percentage that is faith-based. Younger CDFIs are more likely to be *minority-owned or controlled*: while nearly one-quarter (24.2%) of all CDFIs are *minority-owned or controlled*, 30.5% of CDFIs under 5 years old and 38% of CDFIs that are five to 9 years old are *minority-owned or controlled*, as opposed to 14.5% of CDFIs 10 to 17 years of age and 15.3% of CDFIs 18 years or older. Faith-based CDFIs are relatively young with 10.2% of the very youngest CDFIs being faith-based and only 3.4% of the oldest being so. In contrast, nearly one-fourth (23.6%) of CDFIs aged 10 to 17 years are *women-owned or controlled*, as compared to approximately 14% of each of the other age groups.

Table 3-9: Ownership Characteristics of CDFIs by Age of CDFI, FY 2003

 Characteristics of CDFIs by asset size

Looking at type of CDFI by the size of total assets, as shown in Figure 3-4 and Table 3-10, one characteristic is evident. All CDFI banks, regardless of their age, are large due to their regulatory requirements. However, all other types of CDFIs are found in substantial numbers in each of the size categories.

Loan funds represent 88.5% of the smallest CDFIs and this proportion declines to 72.9% of the largest CDFIs. Credit unions are only 5.8% of the smallest CDFIs, and 13.8% and 22.2% respectively for CDFIs with assets of between $1.5 to $4.9, and $5.0 to $14.9 million, but just 8.5% of the largest CDFIs. All CDFI banks have total assets exceeding $15.0 million.

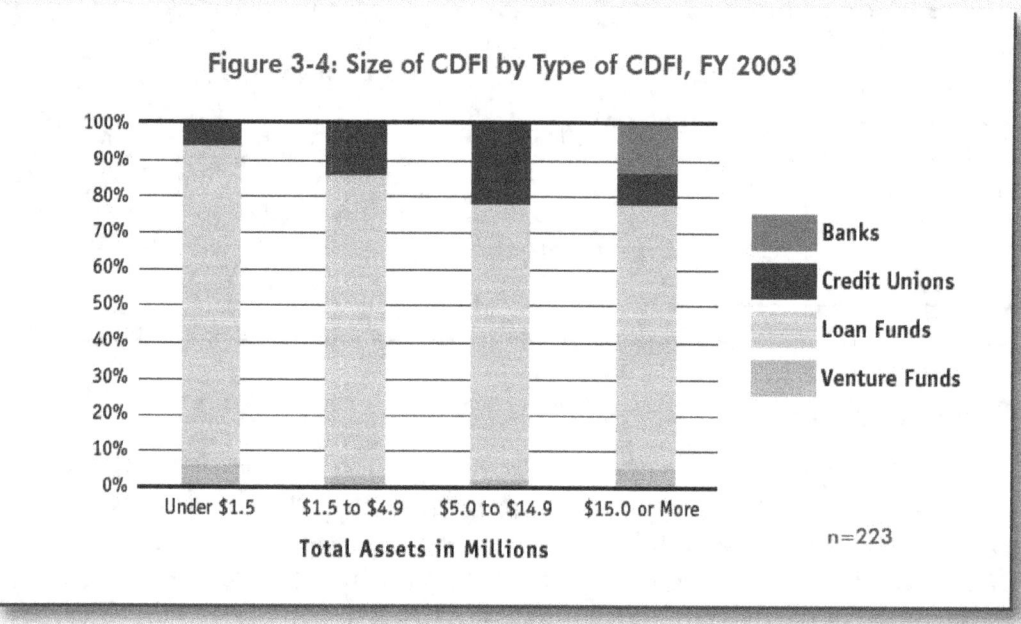

Figure 3-4: Size of CDFI by Type of CDFI, FY 2003

Table 3-10: Size of CDFI by Type of CDFI, FY 2003

	$1.5 Million or Less		$1.5 to $4.9 Million		$5.0 to $14.9 Million		$15.0 Million or more		All CDFIs	
Banks	0	0%	0	0%	0	0%	8	13.6%	8	3.6%
Credit Unions	3	5.8%	8	13.8%	12	22.2%	5	8.5%	28	12.6%
Loan Fund	46	88.5%	48	82.8%	41	75.9%	43	72.9%	178	79.8%
Venture Fund	3	5.8%	2	3.4%	1	1.9%	3	5.1%	9	4%
Total	52	100%	58	100%	54	100%	59	100%	223	100%

 CDFIs of all ages have diverse ownership characteristics.

The ownership characteristics by size of CDFI are summarized in Table 3-11. In terms of minority ownership, the results are very similar to the age analysis findings: minority ownership or control is highest among smaller CDFIs (38.5% of CDFIs with total assets of $1.5 million or less, and 29.3% of CDFIs with total assets of $1.5 to $4.9 million). This percentage declines slightly for CDFIs with total assets between $5 and $14.9 million but then drops sharply for the very largest CDFIs to just 8.5%. In terms of female ownership and faith-based organizations, there is no significant difference across size of CDFI.

Table 3-11: Ownership Characteristics of CDFIs by Size of CDFI, FY 2003

	$1.5 Million or Less	$1.5 to $4.9 Million	$5.0 to $14.9 Million	$15.0 Million or more	All CDFIs
n	52	58	54	59	223
Minority Owned or Controlled	38.5%	29.3%	22.2%	8.5%	24.2%
Women Owned or Controlled	13.5%	19.3%	14.8%	16.9%	16.2%
Faith Based Organization	5.8%	6.9%	9.3%	3.4%	6.3%

 As CDFIs get older, they tend to get larger.

Table 3-12 shows the results of a cross-tabulation between total assets and age. The purpose of a cross-tabulation is two-fold: to determine whether there is any statistically significant relationship between two factors (in other words, these results are not likely to have occurred by chance), and to provide a quantitative measure of this relationship, if one exists. This relationship can be positive or negative: if there is a tendency to see that one factor increases as the other increases, this is said to be a positive relationship, or correlation. If one factor decreases as the other increases, this relationship is said to be a negative one.

The results demonstrate a moderately strong positive relationship between age and size. For instance, among CDFIs with assets under $1.5 million, 65% of the CDFIs of this size have been offering financial services for four years or less. Only 8% of this size is among the oldest group of CDFIs. Conversely, among those CDFIs with the largest assets ($15 million or more), nearly half (46%) have been financing 18 years or more, and another third (34%) have been financing 10 to 17 years. Overall, the relationship is strong and positive (r = .526, p < .001). This relationship is, of course, only a cross-sectional view of the CDFI industry at one point in time. However, the finding suggests that CDFIs are dynamic institutions that grow larger as they mature.

Table 3-12: Relationship between Size and Age of CDFI, FY 2003

| | Age of CDFI | | | | | | | | All CDFIs | |
	4 Years or Less		5 to 9 Years		10 to 17 Years		18 Years or More			
$1.5 Million or Less	34	65%	13	25%	1	2%	4	8%	52	100%
$1.5 to $4.9 Million	14	24%	13	23%	25	43%	6	10%	58	100%
$5.0 to $14.9 Million	7	13%	16	29%	9	17%	22	41%	54	100%
$15.0 Million or more	4	7%	8	13%	20	34%	27	46%	59	100%
Total	59	27%	50	22%	55	24%	59	27%	223	100%

Chi-square = 93.1 p < .001
r = .526 p < .001

Loan and Investment Portfolios

CDFIs finance a wide range of activities, from business development and **commercial real estate** *construction, to home purchase and multi-family housing rehabilitation, to* **community facilities** *construction and student loans. This financing is predominantly in the form of term loans, but also includes lines of credit and equity investments. An examination of CDFIs' loan and equity investment portfolios reveals the proportion of financing that CDFIs are providing to each sector, the type of financing being provided, and the overall amount of financing CDFIs have invested in the communities they serve. The portfolio analysis in this chapter is based on the portfolios outstanding at each CDFI's FY 2003 year end.*

 CDFIs held a portfolio of over \$3.4 billion at the end of FY 2003.

In CIIS, CDFI financing was broken down into six purposes: business development; home purchase and improvement; *commercial real estate* development; housing real estate development; consumer (including automobile purchases, education, and medical care); and other. "Other" is any loan or investment: a) that does not fit into the previous categories; b) that includes multiple purposes; c) for which the CDFI's purpose categories do not match the CIIS purpose categories; or d) for which the CDFI does not track the purpose.

As of the end of FY 2003, 215 CDFIs reported a combined portfolio outstanding of more than \$3.4 billion, for an average portfolio of \$15.4 million per CDFI.[1] Table 4-1 shows the portfolio outstanding by purpose.

---

[1] The data for eight CDFIs are not included in the analysis. Five of these did not provide portfolio data. The other three reported zero financing outstanding. One was a start-up CDFI that had not begun financing activities, another made very short-term loans and had zero loans outstanding at year end, and the last originated loans on its parent's books.

Table 4-1: Portfolio Outstanding by Purpose, FY 2003

	Loans/Investments		Outstanding Balance at Year End	
	Number	Percent	Amount	Percent
Business – Fixed Asset	3,911	5.2%	$234,025,669	6.8%
Business – Working Capital	6,706	9.0%	$222,697,437	6.5%
Subtotal Business	10,617	14.2%	$456,723,107	13.3%
Home Improvement	3,905	5.2%	$63,045,063	1.8%
Mortgage	16,813	22.5%	$994,534,990	29.0%
Subtotal Home	20,718	27.8%	$1,057,580,053	30.8%
Commercial Real Estate Construction	933	1.3%	$191,287,337	5.6%
Commercial Real Estate Rehabilitation	371	0.5%	$83,107,472	2.4%
Subtotal *Commercial Real Estate*	1,304	1.7%	$274,394,809	8.0%
Multi Family Housing Real Estate Construction	467	0.6%	$135,139,486	3.9%
Single Family Housing Real Estate Construction	720	1.0%	$89,431,869	2.6%
Multi Family Housing Real Estate Rehabilitation	1,710	2.3%	$804,157,377	23.4%
Single Family Housing Real Estate Rehabilitation	361	0.5%	$53,674,709	1.6%
Subtotal Residential Real Estate	3,258	4.4%	$1,082,403,441	31.5%
Consumer	31,552	42.3%	$159,345,731	4.6%
Other	7,130	9.6%	$403,264,335	11.7%
Total	74,579	100.0%	$3,433,711,476	100.0%

n = 215

Looking at the table, it is clear that, in dollar terms, these CDFIs concentrate the vast majority of their capital on home purchase (29.0%) and multi-family housing rehabilitation (23.4%). In terms of the number of loans, the largest sectors are consumer (42.3%) and home purchase (22.5%) financing.

Nearly ten percent of the number of loans and investments and nearly 12 percent of the dollar amount are classified as "Other." As will be seen later in this chapter, this is largely due to the bank and credit union portfolios. The way that banks and credit unions classify their loans prevents them from matching a portion of their loans to a CIIS purpose category. Any loan that cannot be classified is entered into CIIS as "Other."

A closer look at the data, however, reveals that two of the outliers identified in Chapter 3, Center for Community Self-Help (Self-Help) and Community Preservation Corporation (CPC), account for nearly half (42%) of the entire portfolio outstanding (see Figure 4-1).[2]

---

[2] The third outlier identified in Chapter 2, Local Initiatives Support Corporation (LISC), also holds a large portfolio ($243.3 million). While LISC's total portfolio is more than 15 times the average for all CDFIs in FY 2003, this figure is only 1.47 standard deviations from this average. As such, it is not an outlier.

Each of the outliers specializes in a single lending purpose: Self-Help specializes in home purchase financing and accounts for 80% of the entire mortgage portfolio reported in Table 4-1. Community Preservation Corporation focuses on multi-family housing rehabilitation and accounts for 71.4% of this portion of the portfolio reported in Table 4-1. When these two outlier organizations are removed, the total portfolio outstanding is $2 billion and its composition is much more evenly distributed across purposes (see Table 4-2).

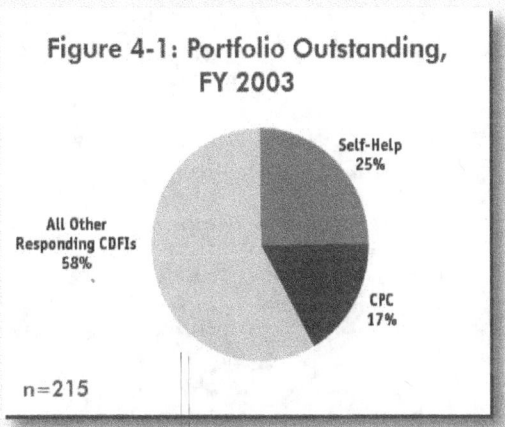

Figure 4-1: Portfolio Outstanding, FY 2003

Self-Help 25%

All Other Responding CDFIs 58%

CPC 17%

n=215

Table 4-2: Portfolio Outstanding by Purpose, Outliers Excluded, FY 2003

	Loans/Investments		Outstanding Balance	
	Number	Percent	Amount	Percent
Business – Fixed Asset	3,840	6.0%	$226,751,575	11.3%
Business – Working Capital	6,588	10.2%	$221,241,899	11.0%
Subtotal Business	**10,428**	**16.2%**	**$447,993,475**	**22.3%**
Home Improvement	3,905	6.1%	$63,045,063	3.1%
Home Purchase	8,057	12.5%	$193,994,597	9.7%
Subtotal Home	**11,962**	**18.6%**	**$257,039,660**	**12.8%**
Commercial Real Estate **Construction**	933	1.4%	$191,287,337	9.5%
Commercial Real Estate **Rehabilitation**	359	0.6%	$69,498,253	3.5%
Subtotal Commercial Real Estate	**1,292**	**2.0%**	**$260,785,590**	**13.0%**
Multi Family Housing Real Estate Construction	457	0.7%	$130,553,557	6.5%
Single Family Housing Real Estate Construction	720	1.1%	$89,431,869	4.5%
Multi Family Housing Real Estate Rehabilitation	700	1.1%	$229,562,331	11.4%
Single Family Housing Real Estate Rehabilitation	361	0.6%	$53,674,709	2.7%
Subtotal Housing Real Estate	**2,238**	**3.5%**	**$503,222,466**	**25.1%**
Consumer	31,552	49.0%	$159,345,731	7.9%
Other	6,931	10.8%	$376,794,930	18.8%
Total	**64,403**	**100.0%**	**$2,005,181,852**	**100.0%**

n = 213

Figures 4-2 and 4-3 show graphically the difference in portfolio composition with and without Self-Help and Community Preservation Corporation.

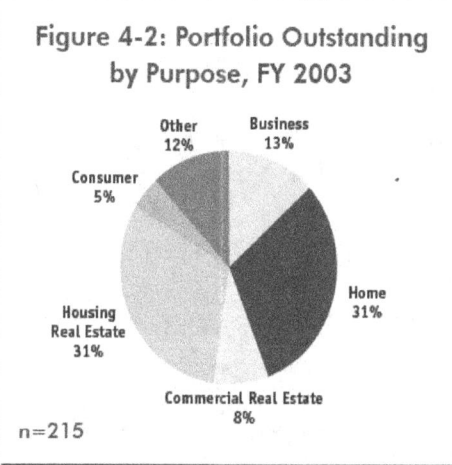

Figure 4-2: Portfolio Outstanding by Purpose, FY 2003

Other 12%
Business 13%
Consumer 5%
Home 31%
Housing Real Estate 31%
Commercial Real Estate 8%

n=215

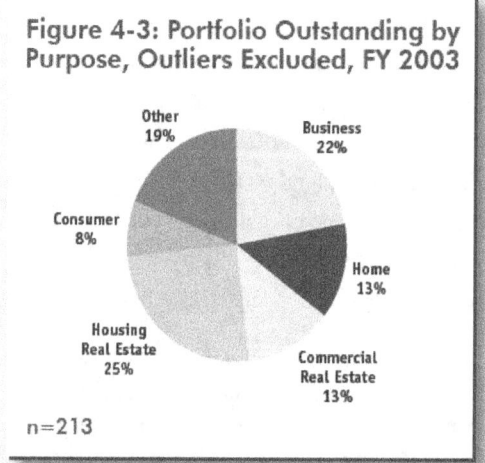

Figure 4-3: Portfolio Outstanding by Purpose, Outliers Excluded, FY 2003

Other 19%
Business 22%
Consumer 8%
Home 13%
Housing Real Estate 25%
Commercial Real Estate 13%

n=213

NOTE: The analysis in the remainder of this chapter includes the outliers except where noted. In many instances, the data are presented with and without the outliers for comparison purposes.

 CDFI loans and investments are located across all regions of the U.S.

Breaking out the portfolio geographically by the headquarters locations of the CDFIs, in Table 4-3, one sees that it is distributed across all of the nine Census Bureau divisions in the country. (In FY 2003, CDFIs did not provide information on the locations of their loans and investments; headquarters address was the best location information available. Starting in FY 2004, location of individual projects financed will begin to be available through the Fund's transaction level data.) Because census divisions are rather large geographical areas (See Figure 4-4), the Fund is reasonably confident that most of the loans and investments are in fact located in the same census division as the headquarters of the CDFI, with the clear exception of the portfolios of the CDFIs that serve a national market.

SeaArk Boats is a boat manufacturer in Monticello, Arkansas. Financing provided by Enterprise Corporation of the Delta, a certified CDFI, kept the company afloat.
SOURCE: Enterprise Corporation of the Delta

Table 4-3: Portfolio Outstanding by CDFI Headquarters, FY 2003

Census Division	Loans/ Investments		Outstanding Balance at Year End	
	Number	Percent	Amount	Percent
New England	5,351	7.2%	$153,122,449	4.5%
Middle Atlantic	12,722	17.1%	$977,484,887	28.5%
South Atlantic	17,471	23.4%	$1,028,411,655	30.0%
East South Central	4,925	6.6%	$194,302,682	5.7%
West South Central	6,706	9.0%	$199,127,967	5.8%
East North Central	4,356	5.8%	$302,226,200	8.8%
West North Central	8,741	11.7%	$243,523,919	7.1%
Mountain	4,265	5.7%	$82,841,278	2.4%
Pacific	10,042	13.5%	$252,670,440	7.4%
Total	74,579	100.0%	$3,433,711,476	100.0%

n = 215

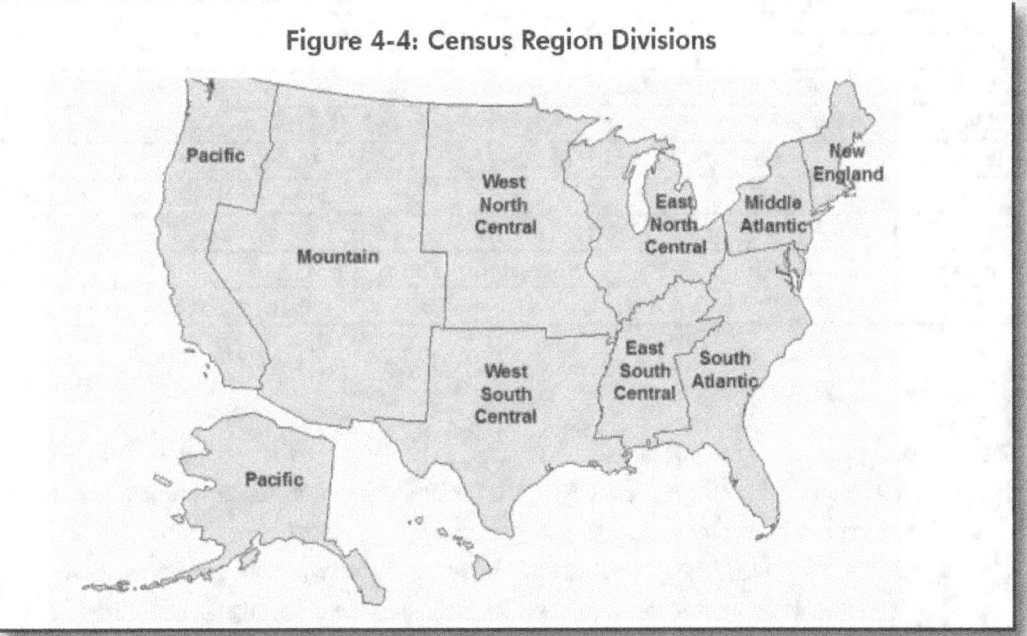

Figure 4-4: Census Region Divisions

In terms of dollar value, the CDFI industry portfolio is especially concentrated in the South Atlantic region (which includes the populous states of Virginia, Florida, Georgia, and North Carolina) and the Mid-Atlantic (New York, New Jersey, and Pennsylvania). Nearly one-third (30.0%) of the portfolio is located in the South Atlantic region (again because one of the largest CDFIs, Self-Help, is headquartered in North Carolina). Another third (28.5%) is in the Mid-Atlantic region, the location of Community Preservation Corporation, another of the largest CDFIs.

**Most financing is in the form of term loans;
equity investments and lines of credit are infrequent.**

The vast majority (83.1%) of transactions are term loans. Only 4.1% are lines of credit, less than one percent (.3%) are equity investments, and 12.4% are reported as other, which includes debt with *equity-like features*. See Table 4-4.

Table 4-4: Portfolio Outstanding by Purpose and Transaction Type, FY 2003

	Business	Home	Commercial Real Estate	Residential Real Estate	Consumer	Other	All Purposes
TERM LOANS							
Number	8,746	19,162	688	2,919	25,160	5,057	61,732
Percent	83.3%	93.0%	53.2%	89.6%	79.7%	71.5%	83.1%
LINES OF CREDIT							
Number	248	146	10	128	2,361	175	3,068
Percent	2.4%	0.7%	0.8%	3.9%	7.5%	2.5%	4.1%
EQUITY INVESTMENTS							
Number	150	0	0	56	0	41	247
Percent	1.4%	0.0%	0.0%	1.7%	0%	0.6%	.3%
OTHER							
Number	1,350	1,294	595	155	4,031	1,798	9,223
Percent	12.9%	6.3%	46.0%	4.8%	12.8%	25.4%	12.4%
TOTAL							
Number	10,494	20,602	1,293	3,258	31,552	7,071	74,270
Percent	100.0%	100.0%	100.0%	100.0%	100.0%	100.0%	100.0%

 Portfolio composition varies by type of CDFI.

Table 4-5 summarizes loans and investments outstanding by purpose for each type of CDFI. The composition of portfolio outstanding differs across CDFI types. Looking at non-regulated institutions first, two types of financing each constitute more than one-third of loan fund portfolios: residential real estate (38.7%) and home financing (36.4%). Three-quarters of venture funds' portfolios support business development. For regulated institutions, the data is less definitive due to the high percentage of financing categorized as other. The reason for the relatively high percentages of other (more than one-third of the bank portfolio and one-fifth of the credit union portfolio) is that regulated institutions do not track many of their loans by the Fund's categories. As a result, a large percentage of other likely includes business, home, real estate and consumer loans. For banks, commercial real estate (20.0%) and business (16.5%) are the second and third largest categories. For credit unions, consumer loans make up nearly 60% of the portfolio.

Table 4-5: Portfolio Outstanding by Type of CDFI and Purpose, FY 2003

	Banks	Credit Unions	Loan Funds	Venture Funds	All CDFIs
n	8	28	171	8	215
Total Amount	$487,694,665	$222,725,239	$2,664,424,452	$58,867,120	$3,433,711,476
Business	16.5%	5.3%	12.0%	75.0%	13.3%
Home	11.1%	14.9%	36.4%	0.0%	30.8%
Commercial Real Estate	20.0%	2.9%	6.2%	11.0%	8.0%
Residential Real Estate	10.3%	0.6%	38.7%	0.0%	31.5%
Consumer	5.9%	58.1%	0.0%	0.0%	4.6%
Other	36.1%	18.2%	6.7%	14.0%	11.7%
Total	100.0%	100.0%	100.0%	100.0%	100.0%

With a combined portfolio outstanding of $2.7 billion, loan funds hold more than three-fourths (77.6%) of the entire industry's portfolio. Even removing the two outliers, loan funds remain the largest portion of the portfolio, with $1.2 billion (61.6%) of $2 billion outstanding. When the outliers are included, loan fund activity is largely concentrated in housing: over one-third (38.7%) of outstanding loans and investments is devoted to housing real estate development and nearly an identical proportion (36.4%) is in home purchase and improvement. Table 4-6 demonstrates that when the outliers are removed, residential real estate remains the largest portion (36.6%) of the portfolio, but it is now followed by business (25.2%). Home purchase and improvement falls to 13.7%, commensurate with commercial real estate and other financing.

Table 4-6: Loan Fund Portfolio Outstanding, Outliers Excluded, FY 2003

	Amount	Percent
Business	$311,336,953	25.2%
Home	$169,598,617	13.7%
Commercial Real Estate	$150,471,442	12.2%
Residential Real Estate	$451,753,201	36.6%
Consumer	$952,151	0.1%
Other	$151,782,464	12.3%
Total	$1,235,894,828	100.0%

n= 169

Figures 4-5 through 4-9 provide a proportionate view of the portfolio outstanding by CDFI type. For loan funds, figures are provided for the portfolio with and without the outliers.

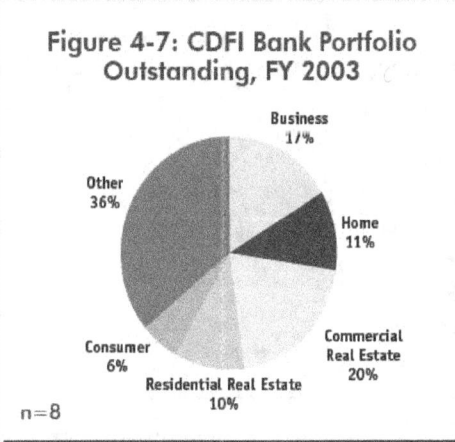

Figure 4-5: Loan Fund Portfolio Outstanding, FY 2003

- Other 7%
- Business 12%
- Consumer 0%
- Residential Real Estate 39%
- Home 36%
- Commercial Real Estate 6%

n=171

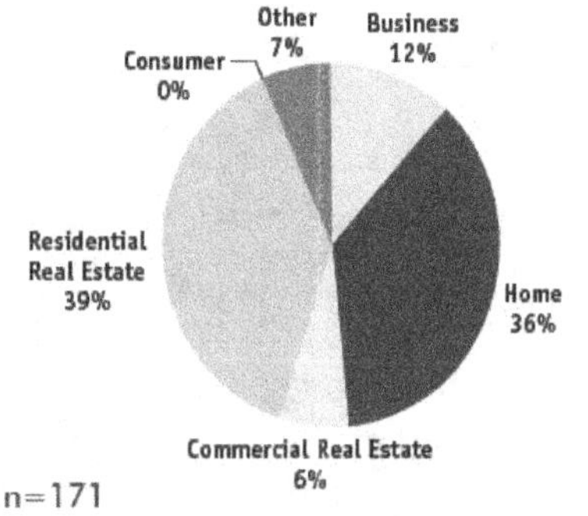

Figure 4-6: Loan Fund Portfolio Outstanding, Outliers Excluded, FY 2003

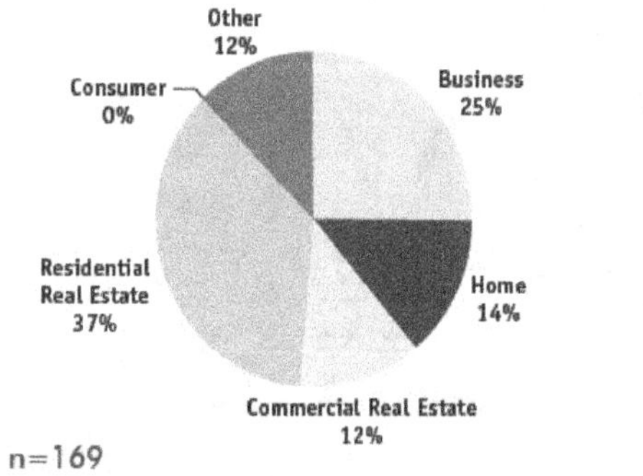

- Other 12%
- Business 25%
- Consumer 0%
- Residential Real Estate 37%
- Home 14%
- Commercial Real Estate 12%

n=169

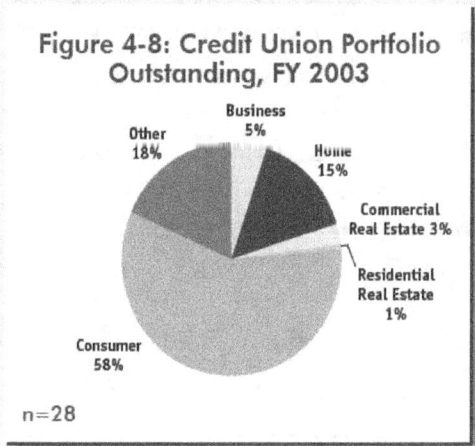

Figure 4-7: CDFI Bank Portfolio Outstanding, FY 2003

- Business 17%
- Other 36%
- Home 11%
- Consumer 6%
- Commercial Real Estate 20%
- Residential Real Estate 10%

n=8

Figure 4-8: Credit Union Portfolio Outstanding, FY 2003

- Business 5%
- Other 18%
- Home 15%
- Commercial Real Estate 3%
- Residential Real Estate 1%
- Consumer 58%

n=28

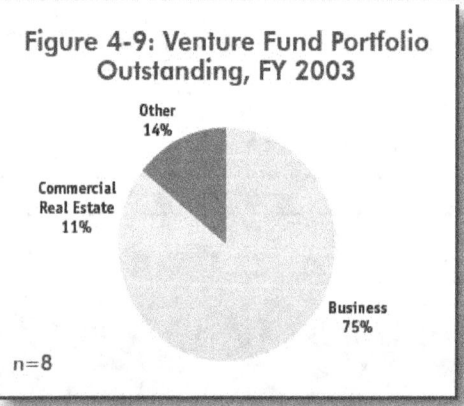

Figure 4-9: Venture Fund Portfolio Outstanding, FY 2003

- Other 14%
- Commercial Real Estate 11%
- Business 75%

n=8

▶ Older CDFIs have larger portfolios.

As one might expect, there is a strong correlation between the age of a CDFI and the number and total amount of loans and investments in its portfolio. Table 4-7 provides a breakdown of the portfolio of all CIIS respondents by both the age of the CDFI and the major purpose of the loan or investment. It should be noted that this is not a trend analysis of the same CDFIs over time; rather, it is a snapshot of different CDFIs at a point in time.

Table 4-7: Portfolio Outstanding by Age of CDFI and Purpose, FY 2003, Outliers Excluded

	4 Years or Less	5 to 9 Years	10 to 17 Years	18 or More Years	All CDFIs
n	59	50	55	59	213
Business	$30,733,932	$87,727,938	$139,800,660	$189,730,945	$447,993,475
Home	$8,174,153	$26,533,073	$82,367,469	$139,964,965	$257,039,660
Commercial Real Estate	$683,736	$18,781,673	$70,148,092	$171,172,089	$260,785,590
Residential Real Estate	$34,558,286	$45,187,870	$86,973,786	$336,502,524	$503,222,466
Consumer	$9,446,711	$3,619,140	$27,373,993	$118,905,887	$159,345,731
Other	$35,338,741	$132,458,281	$109,202,838	$99,795,071	$376,794,930
Total	$118,935,559	$314,307,975	$515,866,837	$1,056,071,481	$2,005,181,852
Business	25.8%	27.9%	27.1%	18.0%	22.3%
Home	6.9%	8.4%	16.0%	13.3%	12.8%
Commercial Real Estate	0.6%	6.0%	13.6%	16.2%	13.0%
Residential Real Estate	29.1%	14.4%	16.9%	31.9%	25.1%
Consumer	7.9%	1.2%	5.3%	11.3%	7.9%
Other	29.7%	42.1%	21.2%	9.4%	18.8%
Total	100.0%	100.0%	100.0%	100.0%	100.0%

Several findings are worthy of emphasis here. First, there is a step-wise progression in the total value of the portfolio in the younger to older CDFIs. The portfolio outstanding for the youngest CDFIs (with just four years or less engaged in financing) was $118.9 million, then increases to $314.3 million, increases again to $515.9 million and finally jumps to over $1 billion in total loans for CDFIs that have been financing 18 years or more.

This overall finding is highlighted in Figure 4-10, which shows the average amount of loans in the portfolio by age of CDFI. Even without the skewing effect of the outliers, the trend is clear. Younger CDFIs with little lending and investing experience have a modest portfolio outstanding. This average more than triples for CDFIs with five to nine years experience and increases noticeably yet again for those CDFIs with between 10 and 17 years of financing. Finally, those CDFIs with the most financing experience on average have much more highly valued portfolios than all younger CDFIs and twice the average of the next youngest group. These relationships are true even when banks are removed from the analysis. They are also true for all financing purposes except consumer and other.

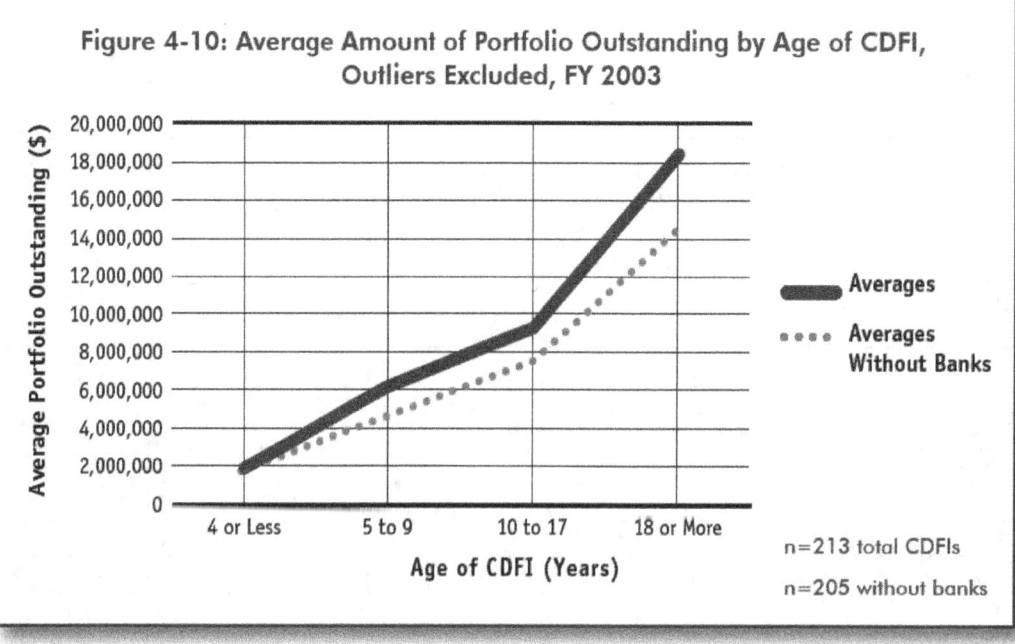

Figure 4-10: Average Amount of Portfolio Outstanding by Age of CDFI, Outliers Excluded, FY 2003

n=213 total CDFIs

n=205 without banks

Capital Under Management

*"Capital under management" is the term used to describe the money that CDFIs have available for lending and investing. Like all financial institutions, CDFIs receive capital from a variety of sources. In fact, because most CDFIs are non-profit institutions and are mission driven, CDFIs have an even wider variety of sources of capital than traditional financial institutions. These sources include banks and private corporations, government (federal as well as state and local), philanthropies and religious organizations, individuals, **government sponsored entities (GSEs)**[1], and internally generated resources. This chapter analyzes the amount, types, sources, and cost of this capital.*

 CDFIs manage over $4 billion in capital and have access to an additional $1 billion in off-balance sheet resources.

A total of 211 CIIS respondents reported $4.2 billion in capital under management in FY 2003.[2] Loan funds manage nearly 75% of this total. See Table 5-1.

Table 5-1: Capital under Management by Type of CDFI, FY 2003

	Banks	Credit Unions	Loan Funds	Venture Funds	All CDFIs
n	7	28	168	8	211
Amount	$743,616,986	$288,204,154	$3,060,168,204	$96,331,919	$4,188,321,263
% of Total	17.8%	6.9%	73.1%	2.3%	100%
Average Per CDFI	$106,230,998	$10,293,006	$18,215,287	$12,041,490	$19,849,864
Median Per CDFI	$105,315,698	$5,132,102	$3,193,173	$6,357,504	$4,180,078

In terms of the average amount of capital under management, banks are the largest with on average $106.2 million. All other types of CDFIs have much smaller amounts of capital under management: credit unions have $10.3 million, loan funds $18.2 million, and venture funds $12.0 million. The median figures for capital under management show just how modest the capital resources of many CDFIs are, and how similar credit unions, loan funds and venture funds are: the median for credit unions is $5.1 million, for loan funds $3.2 million, and for venture funds $6.4 million.

It should be noted that because not all CIIS respondents supplied complete capital under management data, the $4.2 billion undercounts the actual amount for all CIIS respondents.

---

[1]*Government sponsored entities (GSEs)* are privately held corporations with public purposes, created by the U.S. Congress to reduce the cost of capital for certain borrowing sectors of the economy. Members of these sectors include students, farmers and homeowners, among others. GSEs include the Federal Home Loan Banks (FHL Banks), the Federal Home Loan Mortgage Corporation (Freddie Mac), and the Federal National Mortgage Association (Fannie Mae), among others.

[2]The data for 12 CDFIs are not included in the analysis. Ten of these did not provide capital under management data. The other two reported zero capital under management. One was the startup CDFI that had not begun financing activities and the other originated loans on its parent's books. The 211 CIIS respondents that provided usable information include seven of eight banks, all 28 credit unions, 168 of 178 loan funds, and eight of nine venture funds.

In addition to the $4.2 billion in on-balance sheet resources, some CDFIs have access to off-balance sheet capital resources. These off-balance sheet resources total nearly $1 billion and are typically in the form of undrawn lines of credit and, for venture funds, capital that investors have committed to the fund. A breakdown of off-balance sheet resources by type of CDFI is provided in Table 5-2.

Table 5-2: Off-Balance Sheet Resources Available for Lending and Investing, by Type of CDFI, FY 2003

	Banks	Credit Unions	Loan Funds	Venture Funds	All CDFIs
n	8	28	175	9	220
Total Amount	$69,114,243	$1,728,360	$921,300,914	$7,272,500	$999,416,017
% of Total	6.9%	0.2%	92.2%	0.7%	100.0%
Average Per CDFI	$8,639,280	$61,727	$5,264,577	$30,083	$4,542,800
Median Per CDFI	$2,500,000	$0	$50,000	$0	$0

 Eighty percent of capital under management is debt.

Debt constitutes 80.1% of capital under management; equity represents the remaining 19.9%. Table 5-3 provides a breakdown by types of debt and equity.

Table 5-3: Types of Debt and Equity Capital under Management, FY 2003

	Amount	Percent
Debt (excluding EQ2[3] and *Secondary Capital*[4])	$2,364,579,202	56.5%
Deposits and Shares (Depository Institutions)	$915,963,987	21.9%
Equity Equivalent Investments (EQ2)	$67,958,189	1.6%
Secondary Capital	$6,863,376	0.2%
Subtotal Debt	**$3,355,364,754**	**80.1%**
Retained Earnings	$452,559,402	10.8%
Grants	$333,567,051	8.0%
Equity Investments	$46,830,056	1.1%
Subtotal Equity	**$832,956,509**	**19.9%**
Total	**$4,188,321,263**	**100.0%**

n=211

---

[3] Equity equivalent investment (EQ2) is a type of subordinated debt provided by a bank. Among its features, an EQ2 has a rolling term and, therefore, a rolling maturity date.

[4] Secondary capital is a debt instrument available only to credit unions that have an NCUA low-income designation. Secondary capital is defined by NCUA as having several key characteristics, including: being uninsured, being subordinate to all other claims, having a minimum maturity of five years, and not being redeemable prior to maturity.

The largest type of debt, and the one that comprises more than half (56.5%) of all capital under management, is term loans and lines of credit. Bank deposits and credit union shareholder accounts are the second largest source of debt and represent 21.9% of total capital under management. Two other sources of debt, *equity equivalent investments (EQ2)* and *secondary capital,* are specialized debt instruments that make up very small portions of total capital.

Like debt, there are several types of equity included in capital under management, namely: grants to non-profit CDFIs, equity investments in for-profit CDFIs, and retained earnings. Table 5-1 separates equity into these three types, though some explanation is required. Retained earnings (10.8% of total capital under management) are defined as the excess of income over expenses less any dividend payments.[5] Retained earnings are generally earned income, fees and interest income, but also include any unspent grant dollars that a CDFI does not track separately. For example, a CDFI that has small balances from grants received in prior years may not continue to track these balances individually by donor. Rather, the CDFI may account for them as part of retained earnings. Therefore, the table may undercount grants and over count retained earnings.

 Different types of CDFIs rely upon different types of capital.

Table 5-4 summarizes the types of capital under management by type of CDFI. These data underscore the importance of debt as a primary source of capital for all types of CDFIs, with the exception of venture funds. For CDFI banks and credit unions, debt represents more than 90% of their capital under management. For loan funds, debt represents more than three-quarters (77.3%) of their capital. Debt, however, represents less than a third of venture funds' capital (32.9%).

Table 5-4: Debt and Equity Capital under Management, by Type of CDFI, FY 2003[6]

	Banks	Credit Unions	Loan Funds	Venture Funds
n	7	28	168	8
Debt (excluding EQ2 and Secondary Capital)	2.8%	5.3%	75.3%	26.3%
Deposits and Shares (Regulated Financial Institutions)	89.7%	86.2%	NA	NA
Equity Equivalent Investments (EQ2)	NA	NA	2.0%	6.6%
Secondary Capital	NA	2.4%	NA	NA
Subtotal Debt	92.5%	93.8%	77.3%	32.9%
Retained Earnings	5.2%	3.5%	12.2%	32.7%
Grants (to non-profits only)	NA	2.6%	10.5%	6.0%
Equity Investments	2.4%	0.0%	0.1%	28.3%
Subtotal Equity	7.5%	6.2%	22.7%	67.1%
Total	100.0%	100.0%	100.0%	100.0%

---

[5] This definition of retained earnings is not the same as the definition of retained earnings that can be used as matching funds in the Fund's CDFI Program funding applications.

[6] Table totals may be off by .1 due to rounding.

As Table 5-4 shows, types of debt differ between the regulated and unregulated CDFIs. Deposits, understandably, represent the largest type of capital for depository institutions — 89.7% for banks and 86.2% for credit unions. In contrast, term loans and lines of credit are the primary type of capital for loan funds, representing 75.3% of capital under management.

Venture funds, in contrast, rely mostly on equity for their capital under management. Overall, 67.1% of capital is equity, comprised almost equally of retained earnings (32.7%) and equity investments (28.3%).

▶ **Sources of capital vary significantly among types of CDFIs.**

CDFIs borrow capital and receive capital grants and equity investments from a wide range of sources. CIIS provides a source break out of eight categories: depository institutions, corporations, government, *GSEs*, individuals, philanthropy, internal funds[7], and other sources.

Figure 5-1 shows the proportion each source represents of the $4 billion in capital under management. The figure readily shows that private sources are most prevalent, providing 90% of all capital, and that CDFIs do not rely disproportionately on any single source. Depositories are the single largest source, providing nearly one-quarter of all capital. Corporations follow with 16%, and individuals with 12%. Internal funds, *GSEs* and other are each responsible for 10% to 11% of all capital. Only government and philanthropy provide less than 10% of the total (9% and 8%, respectively).

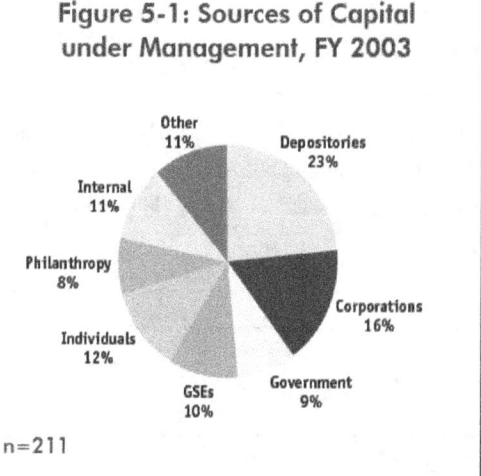

Figure 5-1: Sources of Capital under Management, FY 2003

Other 11%
Depositories 23%
Internal 11%
Philanthropy 8%
Individuals 12%
GSEs 10%
Government 9%
Corporations 16%

n=211

Table 5-5 shows the same information, sources of debt and equity capital, by type of CDFI. It also provides additional detail in three categories. In the table, corporations are subdivided into CDFI intermediaries (CDFIs that invest in other CDFIs), non-depository financial institutions (such as insurance companies, investment banks, pension funds and venture funds, but excluding CDFI intermediaries), and all other corporations, such as real estate developers and utility companies. Government is subdivided into the Fund, other federal agencies, and state and local agencies. Philanthropy is subdivided into non-religious and religious institutions.

The detail in Table 5-5 shows that CDFI intermediaries and non-depository financial institutions provide very small amounts of capital (.5% and 1%, respectively) relative to other corporations (14.6%). Among government sources, the Fund provides just 1.8% of all capital, a small but important amount because it

---

[7]Internal funds includes retained earnings (for-profits and credit unions only) and certain types of net assets (non-profits only) whose specific source cannot be identified.

is primarily difficult-to-find grant and equity capital. Other federal agencies, such as the Small Business Administration (SBA), provide 3.7%, and state and local governments another 3.3% of total capital. Finally, most philanthropic capital comes from non-religious institutions as opposed to religious institutions (6.2% versus 1.3%).

Table 5-5: Sources of Capital under Management by Type of CDFI, FY 2003

	Banks	Credit Unions	Loan Funds	Venture Funds	All CDFIs
n	7	28	168	8	211
Depository Institutions	4.7%	12.4%	29.5%	12.5%	23.5%
CDFI Intermediaries	0.0%	0.6%	0.6%	1.0%	0.5%
Non-Depository Financial Institutions	0.0%	0.0%	1.3%	2.1%	1.0%
All Other Corporations	0.0%	2.4%	19.7%	1.6%	14.6%
Subtotal Corporations	**0.0%**	**3.0%**	**21.6%**	**4.7%**	**16.1%**
CDFI Fund	0.0%	1.1%	2.0%	13.1%	1.8%
Other Federal	0.3%	0.2%	4.9%	5.3%	3.7%
State & Local	4.4%	0.0%	3.3%	4.3%	3.3%
Subtotal Government	**4.7%**	**1.3%**	**10.2%**	**22.7%**	**8.8%**
GSEs	2.2%	1.5%	13.4%	2.1%	10.3%
Individuals	35.5%	68.1%	0.9%	1.2%	11.7%
Non-Religious Institutions	0.0%	0.4%	7.8%	20.7%	6.2%
Religious Institutions	0.0%	0.2%	1.8%	0.5%	1.3%
Subtotal Philanthropy	**0.0%**	**0.6%**	**9.6%**	**21.2%**	**7.5%**
Internal Funds	5.2%	3.5%	12.2%	32.7%	10.8%
Other	47.8%	9.4%	2.7%	3.0%	11.2%
Total	**100.0%**	**100.0%**	**100.0%**	**100.0%**	**100.0%**

Examining these data by type of CDFI reveals that banks rely heavily on individuals (35.5%) and other sources (47.8%). It is important to recognize that banks often cannot separate out their deposits by the categories listed above. Instead, they aggregate deposits from corporations, partnerships and, in some cases, individuals, into other sources. Comparing banks' CIIS data and the data they report to their regulators, it is safe to conclude that banks rely most heavily on individual and corporate depositors for their capital.

Credit unions rely primarily on individual depositors (68.1%), followed by depository institutions (12.4%). It is worth noting that both banks and credit unions have a very small share of their capital from government sources (4.7% and 1.3%, respectively), and that they generate only modest amounts of their total capital from retained earnings and other internal funds (banks at 5.2% and credit unions, just 3.5%).

For loan funds, which are both the most numerous and manage the largest amount of capital, capital is distributed more equitably across different sources, with five of the eight sources each accounting for 10% or more. Depository institutions are the main source, providing nearly one-third (29.5%) of loan funds' capital. Corporations provide another fifth (21.6%) and *GSEs* provide 13.4% followed by internal funds (12.2%) and government (10.2%). The Fund provides 2.0% while federal, state and local government provide 8.2%.

Like loan funds, venture funds rely on a wide range of capital sources. Internal funds were the single most important source of capital under management (32.7%), followed by government (22.7%) and philanthropy (21.2%). Borrowing from depository institutions represents another 12.5%.

The differences in sources of capital across CDFI types are graphically summarized in Figures 5-2 through 5-5.

Figure 5-2: Sources of Capital under Management, Banks, FY 2003

Depositories 5% Government 5% GSEs 2% Other 48% Individuals 35% Internal 5% n=7

Figure 5-3: Sources of Capital under Management, Credit Unions, FY 2003

Other 9% Depositories 12% Internal 4% Philanthropy 1% Corporations 3% Government 1% GSEs 2% Individuals 68% n=28

Figure 5-4: Sources of Capital under Management, Loan Funds, FY 2003

Other 3% Internal 12% Philanthropy 10% Individuals 1% GSEs 13% Government 10% Depositories 29% Corporations 22% n=168

Figure 5-5: Sources of Capital under Management, Venture Funds, FY 2003

Other 3% Depositories 12% Corporations 5% Internal 33% Government 23% GSEs 2% Philanthropy 21% Individuals 1% n=8

 Public sources of capital under management

Our examination of the data on capital under management has demonstrated that public resources are a modest source of capital for the CDFI industry. It is worth examining, through a cross-section of CDFIs by age, whether there is a relationship between the age of a CDFI and government as a source of capital. Do younger CDFIs, for instance, receive a higher proportion of their capital from public sources than older CDFIs or do CDFIs become increasingly dependent upon public sources of capital over time?

Table 5-6 and Figure 5-6 show government sources of capital for CDFIs by age of CDFI. As shown in Table 5-6, the total dollar amount of capital provided by government increases with the age of the CDFI. As shown in the bottom half of Table 5-6 and in Figure 5-6, however, as a percentage of total capital, government sources decrease for the oldest CDFIs. Overall, government capital decreases from 18.1% to 4.5% of total capital for the youngest and oldest CDFIs, respectively. CDFI Fund capital decreases from 6.9% of the youngest CDFIs' capital to less than 1.0% of the oldest CDFIs' capital.

Table 5-6: Government Sources of Capital under Management by Age of CDFI, FY 2003

	4 Years or Less	5 to 9 Years	10 to 17 Years	18 Years or More
n	49	50	53	59
CDFI Fund	$10,017,806	$18,460,797	$28,762,001	$18,422,074
Other Federal	$8,423,014	$41,277,196	$35,872,801	$70,970,437
State and Local	$7,921,331	$41,398,916	$40,018,844	$47,304,042
Subtotal Government	$26,362,151	$101,136,909	$104,653,646	$136,696,553
CDFI Fund	6.9%	4.6%	4.6%	0.6%
Other Federal	5.8%	10.2%	5.8%	2.4%
State and Local	5.4%	10.2%	6.5%	1.6%
Subtotal Government	18.1%	25.0%	16.9%	4.5%

Figure 5-6: Government Sources as a Percent of Total Capital under Management by Age of CDFI, FY 2003

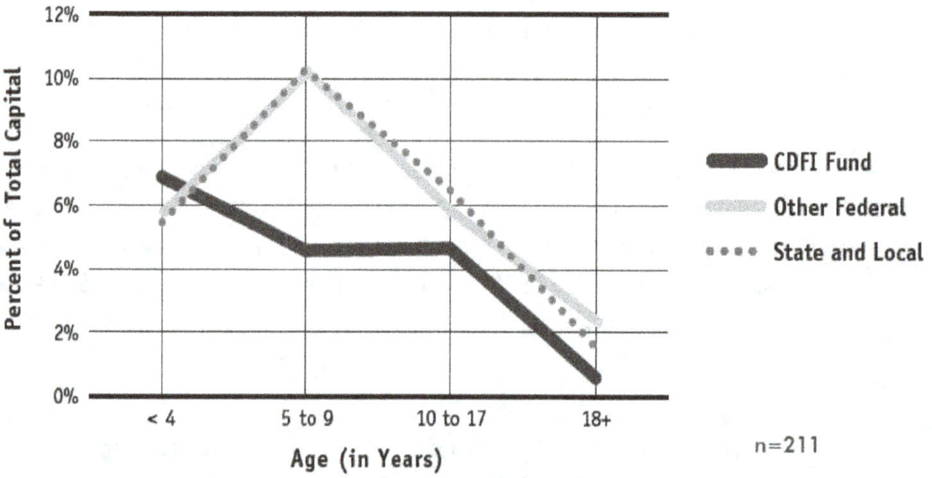

▶ As CDFIs mature, their sources of capital become more diversified.

Loan funds hold nearly three-quarters of the $4.2 billion in capital under management. As the previous analysis showed, loan funds have multiple sources of capital. But is this true for young loan funds as well as mature loan funds? Table 5-7 shows a cross-tabulation between the age of a loan fund (measured by the years of financing) and the number of types of sources of capital. In this table, the various sources of capital are grouped into the eight broad categories used in the figures above. Any one CDFI could have as many as eight distinct sources of capital; however, because very few CDFIs have more than four sources of capital, the number of sources was coded one, two, and so on up to five or more. If a CDFI reports that it received capital from three different banks, it is categorized as having a single source of capital (bank) and is recorded in the first column in the table. If a CDFI reports that it received capital from government and philanthropy, it is categorized as having two sources of capital, and is recorded in the second column. The whole numbers show the number of CDFIs that meet that number of sources criterion in each column.

The finding here is that as loan funds mature and expand their portfolios, they diversify their capital sources, becoming less and less dependent upon only one or two sources: more than 60% of the youngest CDFIs but less than 20% of the oldest CDFIs have only one or two sources of capital. In contrast, nearly 60% of the oldest CDFIs have four or more sources of capital, while this is true for only about 12% of the youngest CDFIs. (See Figure 5-7.) Relying on few sources of capital renders

any financial institution more susceptible to adverse changes in markets or institutional decision-making. For example, foundations often change their focus every few years, so that while community development finance may be a funding priority this year, it may not be next year. Younger, smaller loan funds tend to find themselves in this more precarious position. It should also be recognized that younger CDFIs may not have the capacity to diversify because it takes more human resources than they have available to apply for multiple sources of capital, manage them, and fulfill their annual reporting requirements.

Table 5-7: Relationship between Age of CDFI and Number of Sources of Capital under Management, Loan Funds Only, FY 2003

# of Sources		1	2	3	4	5 or More	All CDFIs
4 Years or Less	n	10	14	13	4	2	43
	% in Row	23.3%	32.6%	30.2%	9.3%	4.7%	100.0%
5 to 9 Years	n	8	8	11	10	7	44
	% in Row	18.2%	18.2 %	25.0%	22.7%	15.9%	100.0%
10 to 17 Years	n	4	12	12	8	10	46
	% in Row	8.7%	26.1%	26.1 %	17.4%	21.7%	100.0%
18 Years or More	n	1	5	6	5	18	35
	% in Row	2.9 %	14.3%	17.1%	14.3%	51.4%	100.0%
Total	n	23	39	42	27	37	168
	% in Row	13.7%	23.2%	25.0%	16.1%	22.0%	100.0%

Pearson's r = .388 p < .001

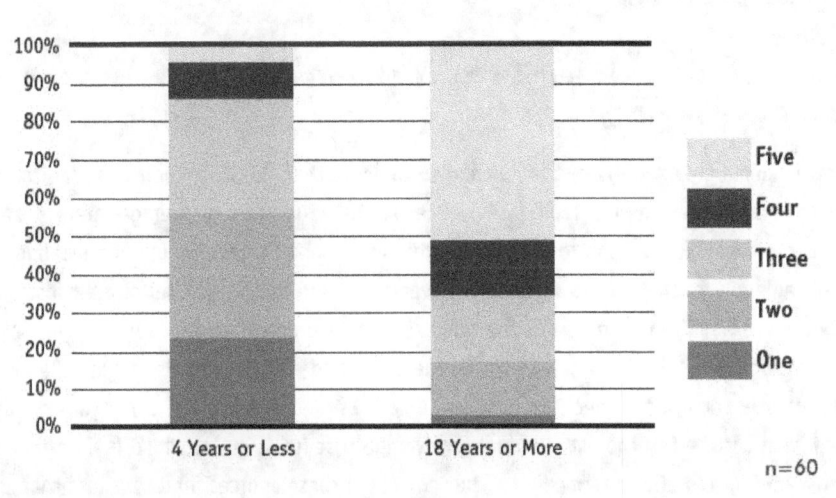

Figure 5-7: Relationship between Age of CDFI and Number of Sources of Capital under Management, Young and Old Loan Funds Only, FY 2003

 The weighted average cost of borrowed capital
is lower for younger CDFIs than older CDFIs.

For each capital loan, the CDFI was asked to report the interest rate and the outstanding balance as of the last day of its FY 2003. A total of 171 CDFIs, the vast majority of which are loan funds, provided sufficient data for the Fund to calculate the weighted average interest rate of borrowed capital. Table 5-8 shows this data by age for all CDFIs and for loan funds only. The rates in the table are for the average CDFI in each group.

Table 5-8 Weighted Average Cost of Borrowed Capital by Age of CDFI, FY 2003

	n	4 Years or Less	5 to 9 Years	10 to 17 Years	18 Years of More
All CDFIs	171				
Average		1.91%	2.24%	2.46%	2.75%
Median		2.00%	2.00%	3.00%	3.00%
Loan Funds Only	148				
Average		1.91%	2.22%	2.40%	2.81%
Median		2.00%	2.00%	3.00%	3.00%

On average, younger CDFIs have lower weighted average costs of capital than older CDFIs. For all CDFIs, the rate is 1.91% for the youngest CDFIs, growing to 2.75% for the oldest CDFIs. For loan funds, the rate starts at 1.91% for the youngest loan funds and grows steadily to 2.81% for the oldest loan funds.

The next section looks at interest rates by source and the interest rates each source charges different age CDFIs. The final sections of this chapter use these data to explain why older CDFIs tend to have higher weighted average costs of capital.

 Government, individuals and philanthropy
provide the lowest cost capital.

The CIIS respondents provided interest rates charged on more than 2,000 of their debt capital instruments. These data are presented in Table 5-9. Sources are listed in order of average interest rate charged, from lowest to highest. In addition to the average, the table shows the minimum and maximum rates as well as the median. Note that all rates are simple averages based on the number of debt instruments held (as opposed to the weighted average). As the table shows, government, individuals and philanthropy fall in the top or lower cost half of the list. Of these, the CDFI Fund and individuals provide the lowest cost capital. At the other end of the spectrum, corporations, *GSEs*, depositories and other sources fall in the bottom or higher cost half of the list. The highest average cost funds are provided by non-depository financial institutions and CDFI intermediaries, but combined these sources represent less than 3.0% of all capital. *GSEs* have the third highest cost.

Table 5-9: Cost of Capital by Source, Loan Funds Only, FY 2003

	n	Mean	Min	Max	Median
1. Government – CDFI Fund	47	1.60%	0.00%	6%	2.00%
2. Individuals	660	1.79%	0.00%	8%	2.00%
3. Government – State and Local	104	2.22%	0.00%	9%	2.00%
4. Philanthropy – Non-Religious	225	2.25%	0.00%	5%	2.00%
5. Philanthropy – Religious	363	2.34%	0.00%	7%	2.00%
6. Government – Other Federal	135	2.41%	0.00%	9%	1.00%
7. Corporations – All Other	45	2.64%	0.00%	8%	2.00%
8. Other	60	2.65%	0.00%	8%	2.00%
9. Depository Institutions	604	3.26%	0.00%	10%	3.00%
10. GSEs	29	3.93%	0.00%	8%	5.00%
11. Corporations – Non-Depository Institutions	21	4.14%	0.00%	6%	4.00%
12. Corporations – CDFI Intermediaries	35	4.46%	1.00%	8%	5.00%
Total	2,328	2.48%	0.00%	10%	2.00%

 Younger CDFIs rely on lower average cost sources of capital than older CDFIs.

Figure 5-8 shows the composition of borrowed capital for the four age groups of CDFIs. As the figure shows, at least half of the capital of the two youngest age groups is provided by philanthropy and government, which are among the lowest cost capital. In contrast, at least half of the capital of the two oldest age groups is provided by depositories and corporations, which are among the higher cost capital. For the oldest CDFIs, *GSEs* – another high cost capital – are the third largest sources.

Figure 5-8: Sources of Borrowed Capital by Age of CDFI, Loan Funds Only, FY 2003

While the difference in average cost of funds per source in and of itself may explain the difference in rates paid by CDFIs of different age groups, a closer look at the data reveals source behavior that makes the differences even larger than initially expected.

▶ **The three sources that older CDFIs rely most heavily on charge higher rates to older CDFIs than to younger CDFIs.**

The three sources that older CDFIs rely most heavily on – corporations, *GSEs*, and depository institutions – all charge higher rates to older CDFIs than to younger CDFIs. Figure 5 - 9 shows this graphically. These data are based on analysis of 678 loans. It should be noted that corporations provided only 49 loans and *GSEs* provided only 39 loans. With so few loans, any generalizations about these sources must be considered tentative.

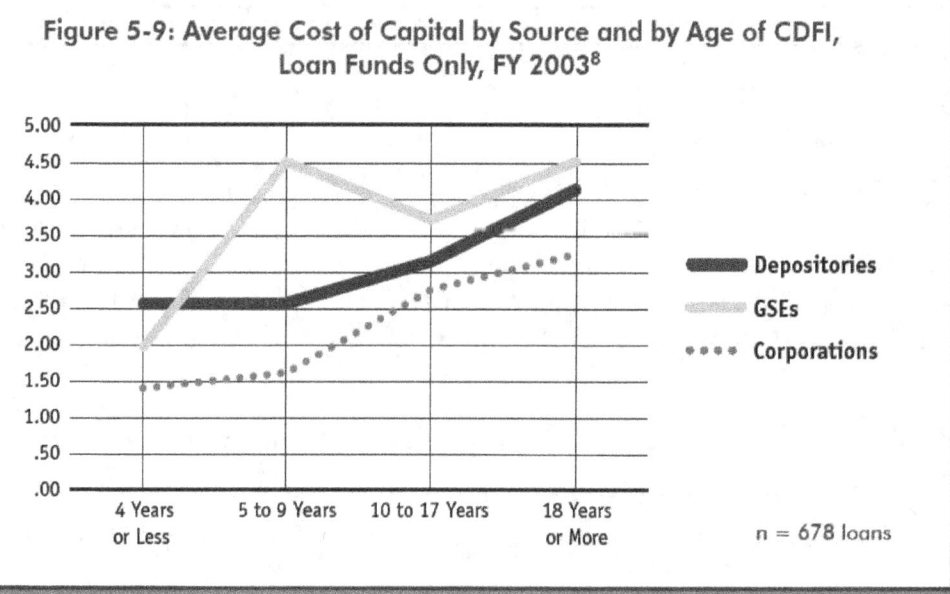

Figure 5-9: Average Cost of Capital by Source and by Age of CDFI, Loan Funds Only, FY 2003[8]

n = 678 loans

The CIIS data do not provide an explanation for why these sources charge more to older CDFIs than to younger CDFIs. However, two possible explanations can be explored: lender policies and the interest rate environment.

Looking at lender policies, it is possible that the observed differences in the average interest rates is due to younger loan funds, in general, and start up loan funds, in particular, receiving a greater portion of

---

[8] *GSEs* made no loans to loan funds that had between 10 and 17 years financing experience; a means substitution (for *GSE* loans) of 3.7% is plotted for this point.

debt at zero interest. Lenders may favor loan funds for zero interest debt because many loan funds are non-profit financial institutions. In addition, philanthropic and other sources may be willing to provide no-interest loans to help emerging institutions get off the ground. Once the institutions mature, these same sources may not be willing to provide such concessionary loan terms. Detailed interest rate data provided by 168 loan funds allows us to examine this hypothesis.

Loan funds report that they paid between zero and 10% for their capital in FY 2003, although only 4.4% of all the loans reported had an interest rate that exceeded 5.0%. To gain a better understanding of which loan funds were paying which rates, borrowed capital under management was divided into five distinct groups according to the interest rate charged (0%, 1%, 2%, 3%, and 4% or more). A cross-tabulation between the age of the loan fund and these interest rate groups of borrowed capital was performed. Figure 5-10 provides a view of these results. The percentages in the bars refer to the amount of capital at each interest rate. The results show that loan funds with four years or less financing experience received almost half (47.4%) of their borrowed capital at zero or 1% interest, and three-fourths (74.8%) at 2% or less. In contrast, one-quarter (24.1%) of the oldest loan funds' borrowed capital had interest rates of 1% or less, and under half (45.4%) had 2% or less. There are even more significant differences at the higher rates. While 14.1% of the youngest loan funds' borrowed capital was at 4% interest or higher, nearly a third (29.3%) of the oldest loan funds' borrowed capital was at these higher rates.

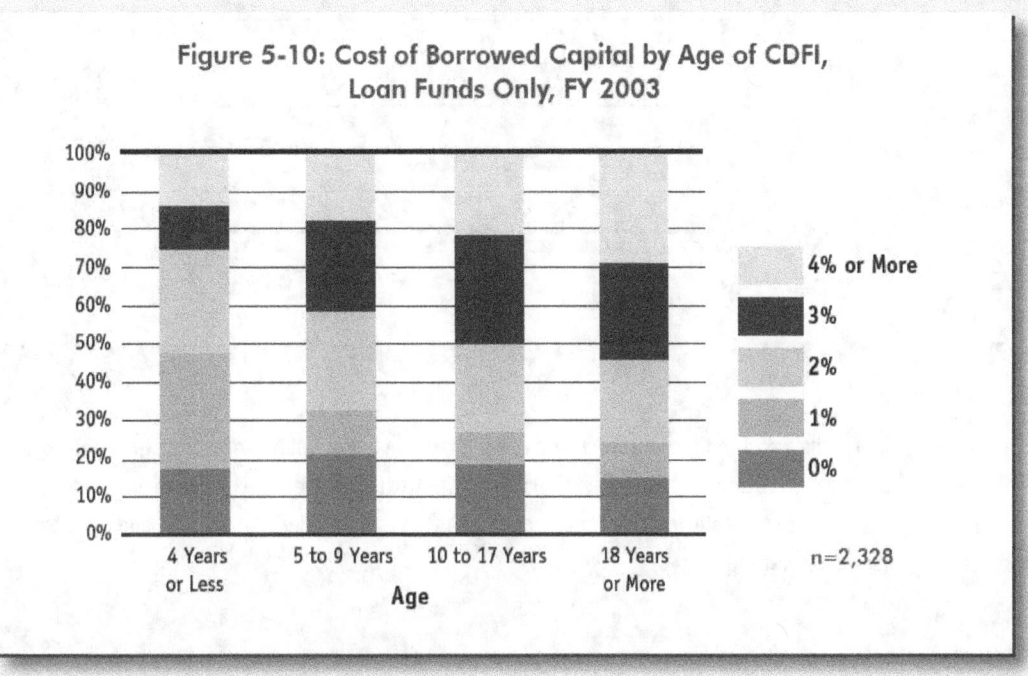

Figure 5-10: Cost of Borrowed Capital by Age of CDFI, Loan Funds Only, FY 2003

▶ **There is a relationship between interest rate environment, age of loan fund, and cost of capital.**

Finally, the analysis turns to the interest rate environment. For purposes of this analysis, the Fund uses the federal funds rate as a proxy for the interest rate environment over time. The federal funds rate is the interest rate at which a depository institution lends immediately available funds (balances at the Federal Reserve) to another depository institution overnight. This is one of the rates that banks use to set the interest rates they charge on their loan products. Figure 5-11 shows the annual average federal funds rate from 1974 to 2004. As the figure shows, interest rates have fluctuated over time with a general downward trend from a high of 16.4% in 1981 to a low of 1.1% in 2003. If interest rate environment is a factor, one can expect to see that a CDFI that borrowed during the eighties paid a higher rate – possibly significantly higher – than a CDFI that borrowed since 2000.

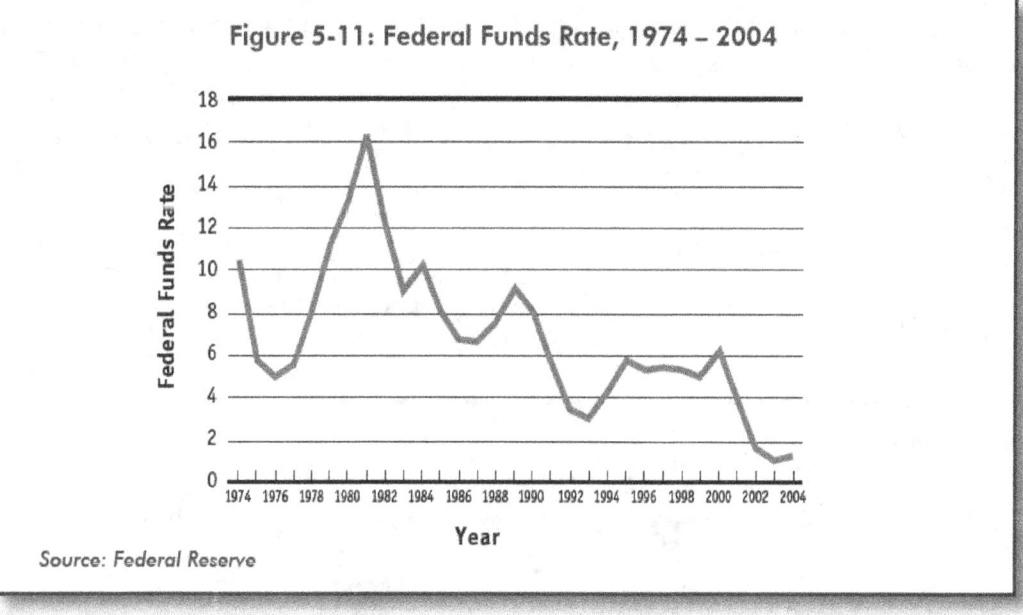

Figure 5-12 shows the weighted average cost of capital for the average CDFI in each age group. This figure is different than previous age figures because it starts with the oldest institutions and ends with the youngest. This order allows for easy comparison between the federal funds rate and the cost of capital by age of loan fund.

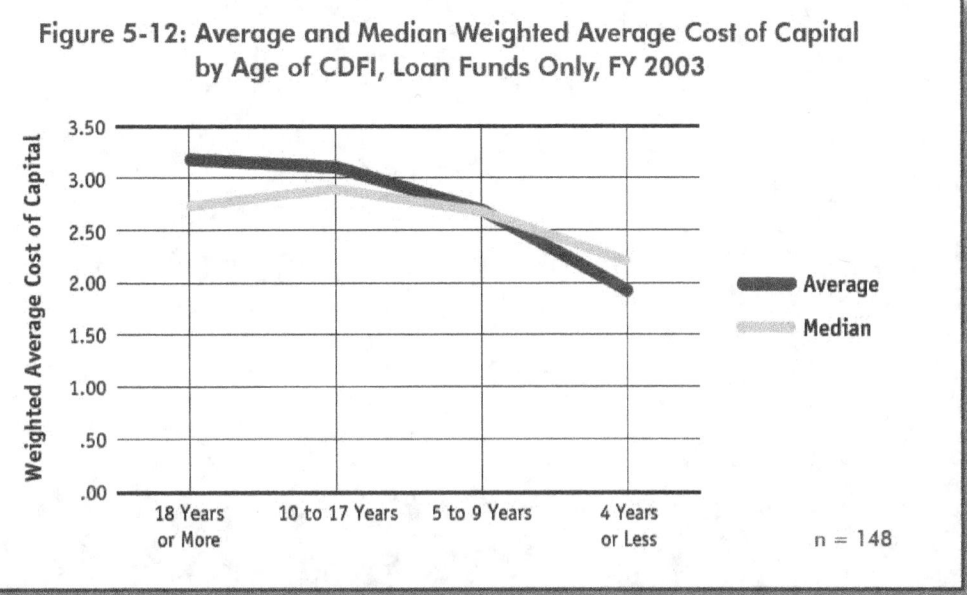

Figure 5-12: Average and Median Weighted Average Cost of Capital by Age of CDFI, Loan Funds Only, FY 2003

The finding portrayed here is consistent with the idea that interest rate environment affects the cost of capital: older loan funds, which may have long-term debt that originated before 2000, have a higher weighted average cost of capital than younger loan funds. Loan funds with 18 years or more experience started financing earlier than 1987. On average, their weighted average cost of capital was 3.18%. Loan funds with 10 to 17 years of financing – debt originated 1987 or later - paid 3.09% to borrow capital. Loan funds with five to nine years experience in financing – whose debt originated in 1995 or later - paid on average 2.68%. The very youngest loan funds – whose oldest debt originated in 2000 or later – had a weighted average cost of capital of 1.92%.

The Fund's analysis of the interest rate environment comes with two caveats. CIIS did not collect the origination date of borrowed capital. Nor did it collect refinancing information. CDFIs – like other borrowers - would likely try to refinance their higher cost debt when interest rates fall. Only if they are unable to refinance would the interest rate environment theory be plausible. In the future, CIIS will collect origination dates for borrowed capital.

Note: This page left blank intentionally.

Operating Revenue

CDFIs not only require capital to provide financing to the low-income and economically distressed areas they serve; all CDFIs also require operating revenue to cover their day-to-day operating costs, such as salaries, rent and utilities.

There are two sources of operating revenue: earned and contributed. Earned revenue is income CDFIs generate from their business activities. This includes portfolio income such as interest and fees earned on loans, and contract, training and consulting fees. Contributed revenue includes grants or in-kind donations from philanthropies, religious institutions, government agencies, private corporations, individuals, and others.

 Regulated CDFIs earn a greater proportion of their operating revenue than do unregulated CDFIs.

There is a striking difference between the average regulated and unregulated CDFI's proportion of earned and contributed operating revenue. On average, banks and credit unions earn nearly all of their operating revenue while unregulated CDFIs, loan funds in particular, receive a significant proportion in contributions.

Table 6-1 shows the percent of the average CDFI's operating income that is earned. The table shows this information by type and age of CDFI. Age data cannot be reported for the oldest venture funds because there are too few institutions reporting.[1]

Table 6-1: Average Earned Revenue as a Percentage of Total Operating Revenue by Type and Age of CDFI, FY 2003

	n	4 Years or Less	5 to 9 Years	10 to 17 Years	18 Years or More	All CDFIs
Banks	8	97%	100%	100%	97%	98%
Credit Unions	28	57%	79%	100%	96%	90%
Loan Funds	178	37%	42%	48%	55%	45%
Venture Funds	9	38%	88%	*	*	65%
Total	223	40%	47%	53%	71%	53%

Overall, banks and credit unions earned an average of 98% and 90%, respectively, of their operating revenue[2]; for loan funds, the comparable figure was 45% and, for venture funds, 65%.

---

[1] When there are two or fewer loan funds or venture funds reporting, the data is suppressed. This rule does not apply to banks and credit unions because their individual financial data is publicly available.

[2] The only source of contributed revenue reported by banks was the CDFI Fund. This may include BEA Program awards as well as CDFI Program awards.

Looking at differences by age group, only loan funds show a clear trend. The percentage of earned income rises steadily across age groups, from 37% for the youngest loan funds to 55% for the oldest.[3]

▶ **Portfolio interest is the largest source of earned revenue for all types of CDFIs.**

For all types of CDFIs, including venture funds, loan portfolio interest accounts for more than half of all earned income. See Table 6-2. Fee income from lending portfolio and retail financial services, which includes loan origination, service and late fees, points, and all account and transaction fees, is the second largest source of income for the regulated institutions, accounting for 16.3% of credit union income and nearly one-fifth (19.5%) of bank's income. Fee income is notably smaller for loan funds (9.0%) and credit unions (1.3%). Loan funds' second largest source of earned revenue is "other", which includes loan servicing fees, loan packaging fees, and rental income from leased properties. For venture funds, interest earned on cash and marketable securities is the second largest source of earned income.

Table 6-2: Sources of Earned Revenue by Type of CDFI, FY 2003

	Banks	Credit Unions	Loan Funds	Venture Funds	All CDFIs
n	8	28	178	9	223
Interest Income Earned on Portfolio	55.5%	73.1%	61.7%	54.6%	61.3%
Fee Income Earned from Lending Portfolio and Retail Financial Services	19.5%	16.3%	9.0%	1.3%	11.2%
Interest Earned on Cash and Marketable Securities	17.0%	6.4%	5.5%	22.2%	7.8%
Contract and Training Income	6.0%	1.2%	7.2%	15.3%	6.7%
Other Earned Revenue	2.0%	3.0%	16.6%	6.5%	13.0%
Total	100.0%	100.0%	100.0%	100.0%	100.0%

Because loan funds constitute such an important part of the CDFI industry, it is worth examining how one relationship changes over time, namely the relationship between portfolio interest income and contributed revenue. As Table 6-1 showed, earned revenue grows from 37% to 55% by age of CDFI. Table 6-3 shows that it is the dramatic increase in portfolio interest income that supports this growth in earned revenue. While between one-third and nearly one-half of younger loan funds' earned revenue comes from portfolio interest, this figure is nearly 70% for the oldest loans funds.

---

[3] This analysis includes the 3 loan funds identified as outliers in previous chapters because the results are not statistically different when these loan funds are removed.

Table 6-3: Sources of Earned Revenue by Age of CDFI, Loan Funds Only, FY 2003

	4 Years or Less	5 to 9 Years	10 to 17 Years	18 Years or More	All CDFIs
n	51	44	48	35	178
Interest Income Earned on Portfolio	37.6%	47.2%	41.2%	69.7%	61.7%
Fee Income from Lending Portfolio	17.2%	8.8%	21.7%	5.5%	9.0%
Interest on Marketable Securities	13.2%	9.7%	10.6%	3.4%	5.5%
Contract and Training Income	21.8%	12.1%	14.6%	4.0%	7.2%
Other Earned Income	10.1%	22.2%	11.9%	17.4%	16.6%
Total	100.0%	100.0%	100.0%	100.0%	100.0%

In other words, only loan funds that have been able to both increase the size of their portfolio and capture the interest income from that portfolio are able to decrease their reliance on contributed revenue.

This chapter continues with an analysis of contributed operating revenue.

Contributed operating revenue comes largely from government, philanthropy, and corporations.

Contributed operating revenue is particularly important for unregulated CDFIs. Private sources provide more than half (55.7%) of all contributions. Federal, state and local governments provide the remainder (44.3%). Overall, two sources stand out: the Federal government, including the Fund, provides more than one-third (35.1%) of all contributions and philanthropy provides one-quarter[4]. The third largest source, corporations (including real estate companies, utilities, insurance companies, investment banks, pension funds, and venture funds), provides 16.3% of all contributions. Among public sources, the Fund is relatively small at 5.1%. Table 6-4 details the amounts provided by each source.

---

[4] Contributions include grants only. They do not include loans, such as those provided by the CDFI Fund and the low-interest Program Related Investments (PRIs) provided by some foundations.

Table 6-4: Sources of Contributed Operating Revenue, FY 2003

	Total Dollars	Percent
PRIVATE		
Depository Institutions	$8,360,270	3.4%
CDFI Intermediaries	$262,216	0.1%
Corporations	$40,512,450	16.3%
GSEs	$4,648,773	1.9%
Individuals	$3,044,464	1.2%
Philanthropy	$63,709,346	25.6%
Other	$17,904,544	7.2%
Subtotal Private	**$138,442,063**	**55.7%**
PUBLIC		
CDFI Fund	$12,727,838	5.1%
Government, Other Federal	$74,606,601	30.0%
Government, State & Local	$22,798,237	9.2%
Subtotal Public	**$110,132,676**	**44.3%**
Total	**$248,574,739**	**100.0%**

n=187[5]

Figure 6-1 shows graphically the proportional share of each source and demonstrates that the CDFI industry is not primarily or overly dependent upon any one source for their contributed operating revenue.

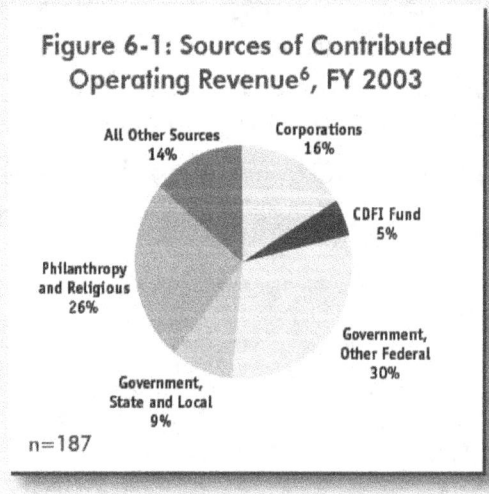

Figure 6-1: Sources of Contributed Operating Revenue[6], FY 2003

n=187

---

[5] Thirty-six organizations did not submit information on their sources of contributed operating revenue. These organizations were excluded from this analysis.

[6] "All Other Sources" combines banks, CDFI intermediaries, individuals, *GSEs*, and other sources, each of which is shown separately in Table 6-4.

 Sources of contributed operating revenue vary by type of CDFI.

Table 6-5 summarizes contributed operating revenue by source for each type of CDFI. For two types of CDFIs – banks and venture funds — the public sector is the primary source of contributions. In fact, for banks, all of which are for-profit institutions which do not qualify for tax-deductible charitable contributions, the Fund is the only source of contributions. Venture funds rely primarily on other federal funds. Credit unions rely most heavily on other private funds followed by the federal government and philanthropy. Loan funds follow the trend described above for all CDFIs: federal government is the largest contributor, followed by philanthropy and corporations.

Table 6-5: Sources of Contributed Operating Revenue by Type of CDFI, FY 2003

	Banks	Credit Unions	Loan Funds	Venture Funds
n	3	10	169	5
Depository Institutions	0.0%	2.7%	3.4%	0.0%
CDFI Intermediaries	0.0%	1.0%	0.1%	1.1%
Corporations	0.0%	1.8%	16.7%	0.2%
GSEs	0.0%	2.0%	1.9%	0.0%
Individuals	0.0%	0.3%	1.3%	0.0%
Philanthropy	0.0%	17.3%	26.0%	10.4%
Other	0.0%	33.9%	7.1%	0.0%
Subtotal Private	0.0%	59.0%	56.4%	11.6%
CDFI Fund	100.0%	7.2%	4.8%	4.7%
Government, Other Federal	0.0%	25.1%	29.6%	73.5%
Government, State & Local	0.0%	8.7%	9.2%	10.1%
Subtotal Public	100.0%	41.0%	43.6%	88.4%
Totals	100.0%	100.0%	100.0%	100.0%

n=187

 Federal government, philanthropic institutions, and corporations are important sources of contributed operating revenue regardless of the age of the CDFI.

Table 6-6 summarizes the sources of contributed operating revenue by the age of the CDFI. These data are provided as an average percentage of contributed operating revenue per CDFI in each age group. Because contributions are such a small proportion of regulated institutions' operating revenue (1.4% for banks and 7.9% for credit unions), the age analysis is limited to loan funds and venture funds.

Looked at in this way, it is easy to identify several findings. First, depository institutions are important sources only for the youngest CDFIs, providing 15.1%. Depository institutions were the source of less than 4% of the revenues of all older CDFIs. Second, two of the three largest sources, government and corporations, become more important as CDFIs age. Corporate support more than triples, growing from 7.5% to nearly a quarter (24.6%) of all contributions. And government support grows from one-third (34.6%) to nearly one-half (44.9%) of contributed revenue. Philanthropic support for CDFIs is not directly related to the age of the CDFI: Philanthropic institutions provide nearly a third of the revenues of the youngest CDFIs and CDFIs with 10 to 17 years of experience (30.5% and 31.3%, respectively), but lesser amounts to other CDFIs, including the oldest where philanthropic contributions represent less than a quarter of their resources (23.8%).

Table 6-6: Sources of Contributed Operating Revenue by Age of CDFI, Loan Funds and Venture Funds Only, FY 2003

	4 Years or Less	5 to 9 Years	10 to 17 Years	18 Years or More
n	55	43	49	40
Depository Institutions	15.1%	3.6%	2.6%	2.6%
CDFI Intermediaries	0.3%	0.0%	0.2%	0.0%
Corporations	7.5%	3.9%	10.3%	24.6%
GSEs	3.1%	2.8%	4.4%	0.0%
Individuals	1.9%	0.8%	1.5%	1.1%
Philanthropy	30.5%	19.9%	31.3%	23.8%
Other	7.0%	5.8%	14.7%	2.9%
Subtotal Private	**65.4%**	**36.8%**	**65.1%**	**55.1%**
CDFI Fund	16.7%	11.6%	2.8%	2.8%
Government, Other Federal	12.7%	37.0%	23.1%	34.0%
Government, State & Local	5.2%	14.6%	9.0%	8.1%
Subtotal Public	**34.6%**	**63.2%**	**34.9%**	**44.9%**
Total	**100.0%**	**100.0%**	**100.0%**	**100.0%**

n=174

Looking more closely at government support, state and local as well as federal support grow with CDFI age. But while federal support from agencies other than the Fund nearly triples, from 12.7% to 34.0%, Fund support falls as CDFIs mature. In fact, the Fund is a significant source of operating revenue only for CDFIs in the two youngest age categories (16.7% and 11.6%, respectively); it accounts for less than 3.0% of support for CDFIs that are 10 years of age or older.

Figure 6-2 shows graphically the change in the percent contribution of each public sector category (Fund, other federal agencies, state and local governments).

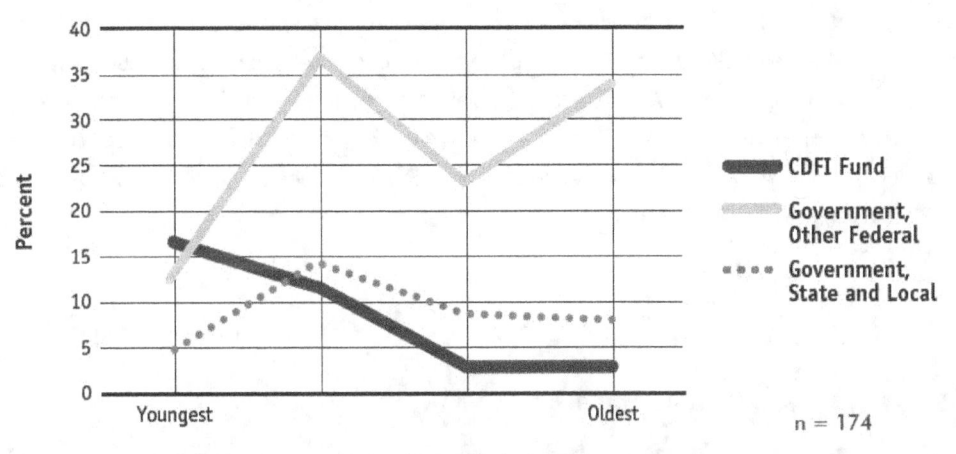

Figure 6-2: Government Sources as a Percent of Total Contributed Operating Revenue by Age of CDFI, Loan Funds and Venture Funds Only, FY 2003

 The age of CDFI and the number of sources of contributed operating revenue are positively related.

Just as older CDFIs are more likely to have more than one or two sources of lending and investment capital, so too do older loan funds and venture funds obtain operating contributions from multiple sources. However, the relationship is not as strong as with capital. See Table 6-7.

Table 6-7: Relationship between Age of CDFI and the Number of Types of Sources of Contributed Operating Revenue, Loan Funds and Venture Funds Only, FY 2003

		1 Source	2 Sources	3 Sources	4 Sources	5 or More Sources	All Sources
4 Years or Less	n	20	11	6	12	2	51
	% in Row	39.2%	21.6%	11.8%	23.5%	3.9%	100.0%
5 to 9 Years	n	8	9	10	9	5	41
	% in Row	19.5%	22.0%	24.4%	22.0%	12.2%	100.0%
10 to 17 Years	n	12	9	12	5	11	49
	% in Row	24.5%	18.4%	24.5%	10.2%	22.4%	100.0%
18 Years or More	n	2	8	6	7	10	33
	% in Row	6.1%	24.2%	18.2%	21.2%	30.3%	100.0%
Total	n	42	37	34	33	28	174
	% in Row	24.1%	21.3%	19.5%	19.0%	16.1%	100.0%

Pearson's r = .264 p < .001

The cross tabulation between the age of CDFIs and the number of sources of operating revenue shows that there is a modest positive relationship between these two variables ($r = .264$). The findings show that 39.2% of the youngest CDFIs obtain their contributed operating revenue from a single type of source (corporations, for example) while only 3.9% have five or more types of sources. On the other hand, 30.3% of the oldest CDFIs have five or more types of contributed operating revenue sources and only 6.1% have a single source. A similar cross tabulation between the size of CDFI and the number of type of sources of contributions provides very similar results: there is a modest positive relationship between the size of a CDFI and the likelihood that the CDFI has a larger number of sources of contributed operating revenue.

Loans and Investments Originated

*In FY 2003, CDFIs originated $1.7 billion in new loans and equity investments. Loan funds were responsible for the largest portion of originations, following closely by banks. FY 2003 originations were largely housing real-estate and business loans. The portfolio outstanding of CDFIs shares these basic purposes but has a higher proportion of **commercial real estate** development and somewhat more in direct business lending. Fundamentally, however, FY 2003 industry originations and portfolio outstanding are quite similar.*

 Housing real estate development represents the largest share of loan and investment originations in FY 2003.

Table 7-1 summarizes loans and investments originated by purpose. The table presents both the dollar value and number of originations. In terms of dollar value, housing real estate construction and rehabilitation represent nearly half (47.8%) of originations. At nearly one-third (32.2%) of all originations, the rehabilitation of multi-family housing is the single most important objective within housing real estate financing. Business loans and investments are the second largest category (18.2%), and they are split almost evenly between fixed asset and working capital loans. Home purchase and improvement is the third largest category, representing almost 10% of all originations. *Commercial real estate* development represents a small but significant share (7.8%).

It should be noted that "Other" accounts for nearly 10% of all originations. Other includes loans and equity investments that were either used for multiple purposes or did not fit into any of the identified purposes. Examples include an investment used for construction of retail space and business loans to the occupants, and an equity investment in a business.

Table 7-1: Loans and Equity Investments Originated by Purpose, FY 2003

	Amount Originated	Percent	Number Originated	Percent
Business – Fixed Asset	$149,034,308	8.8%	2,526	6.6%
Business – Working Capital	$158,619,739	9.4%	4,189	10.9%
Subtotal Business	**$307,654,047**	**18.2%**	**6,715**	**17.5%**
Home Improvement	$21,320,075	1.3%	1,377	3.6%
Home Purchase	$146,418,090	8.7%	3,855	10.1%
Subtotal Home	**$167,738,165**	**9.9%**	**5,262**	**13.7%**
Real Estate Construction, Commercial	$86,665,597	5.1%	533	1.4%
Real Estate Rehabilitation, Commercial	$44,370,953	2.6%	111	0.3%
Subtotal *Commercial Real Estate*	**$131,036,550**	**7.8%**	**644**	**1.7%**
Real Estate Construction, Multi-Family	$105,575,523	6.3%	224	0.6%
Real Estate Construction, Single Family	$88,011,885	5.2%	761	2.0%
Real Estate Rehabilitation, Multi-Family	$543,231,763	32.2%	635	1.7%
Real Estate Rehabilitation, Single Family	$69,835,881	4.1%	512	1.3%
Subtotal Residential Real Estate	**$806,655,052**	**47.8%**	**2,132**	**5.6%**
Consumer	$116,160,602	6.9%	22,177	57.9%
Other	$158,795,683	9.4%	1,401	3.7%
Total	**$1,688,040,099**	**100.0%**	**38,331**	**100.0%**

n=208[1]

As with portfolio outstanding, two CDFIs account for a large portion of originations. Self-Help and Community Preservation Corporation combined account for 29.1% of total originations, including 88.6% of multi-family housing rehabilitation. Table 7-2 provides a summary of FY 2003 originations by purpose, with Self-Help and Community Preservation Corporation excluded. The data in this table allow us to get a more balanced view of the loans and investments the typical CDFI made in FY 2003.

---

[1]The data for 15 CDFIs are not included in the table. Ten of these did not provide portfolio data. The other 5 reported zero financing outstanding. Three had not begun financing activities. One made no loans due to lack of funding. The last organization originated loans on its parent's books.

Table 7-2: Loans and Equity Investments Originated by Purpose, Outliers Removed, FY 2003

	Amount Originated	Percent	Number Originated	Percent
Business – Fixed Asset	$134,117,313	11.2%	2,488	6.6%
Business – Working Capital	$157,007,619	13.1%	,199	10.9%
Subtotal Business	**$291,124,932**	**24.3%**	**6,607**	**17.4%**
Home Improvement	$21,320,075	1.8%	1,377	3.6%
Home Purchase	$146,418,090	12.2%	3,885	10.2%
Subtotal Home	**$167,738,165**	**14.0%**	**5,262**	**13.9%**
Real Estate Construction, Commercial	$86,665,597	7.2%	533	1.4%
Real Estate Rehabilitation, Commercial	$25,634,307	2.1%	105	0.3%
Subtotal *Commercial Real Estate*	**$112,299,904**	**9.4%**	**638**	**1.7%**
Real Estate Construction, Multi-Family	$101,291,423	8.5%	220	0.6%
Real Estate Construction, Single Family	$88,011,885	7.4%	761	2.0%
Real Estate Rehabilitation, Multi-Family	$104,583,223	8.7%	398	1.0%
Real Estate Rehabilitation, Single Family	$69,835,881	5.8%	512	1.4%
Subtotal Residential Real Estate	**$363,722,412**	**30.4%**	**1,891**	**5.0%**
Consumer	$116,160,602	9.7%	22,177	58.5%
Other	$145,803,558	12.2%	1,346	3.5%
Total	$1,196,849,573	100.0%	37,921	100.0%

n=206

The data summarized in Table 7-2 is strikingly different in one way. Housing real estate construction and rehabilitation declines significantly from nearly half of all loans and investments originated to just under a third (30.4%). As expected, this decrease is almost entirely due to multi-family real estate rehabilitation, which falls from nearly one-third (32.2%) to 8.7% of all originations. With the outliers' data removed, working capital and fixed asset business loans and investments increase to almost a quarter (24.3%) of the value of all originations. Figures 7-1 and 7-2 show these comparisons through pie charts.

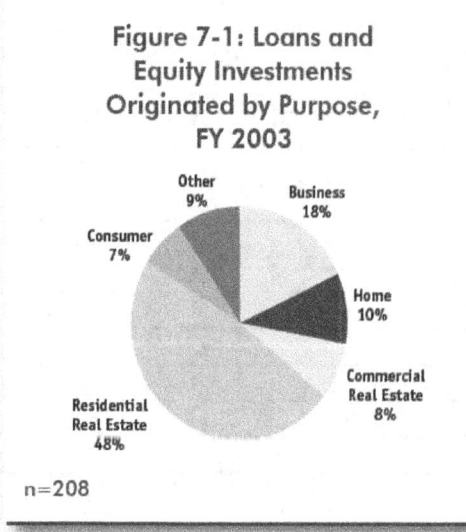

Figure 7-1: Loans and Equity Investments Originated by Purpose, FY 2003

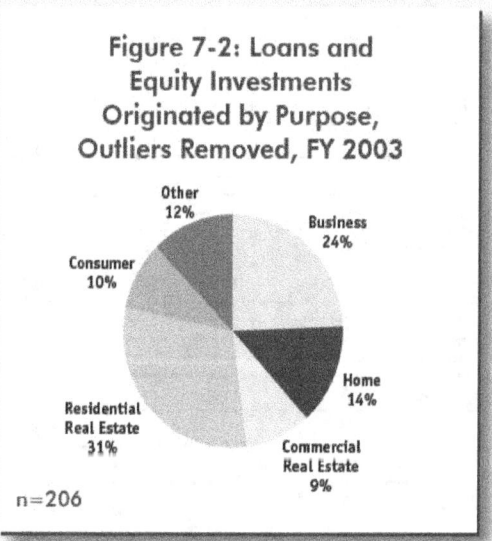

Figure 7-2: Loans and Equity Investments Originated by Purpose, Outliers Removed, FY 2003

 Loans and equity investments originated in FY 2003 are very similar to CDFI portfolio outstanding.

Table 7-3 shows a comparison of portfolio outstanding and originations, by major purpose. The outliers have been removed. As the table shows, originations are proportionately quite similar to the portfolio outstanding.

Table 7-3: Comparison of Portfolio Outstanding and Originations by Purpose, Outliers Removed, FY 2003

	Portfolio Outstanding		Originations	
	Amount	Percent	Amount	Percent
Business	$447,993,475	22.3%	$291,124,932	24.3%
Home	$257,039,660	12.8%	$167,738,165	14.0%
Commercial Real Estate	$260,785,590	13.0%	$112,299,904	9.4%
Residential Real Estate	$503,222,466	25.1%	$363,722,412	30.4%
Consumer	$159,345,731	7.9%	$116,160,602	9.7%
Other	$376,794,930	18.8%	$145,803,558	12.2%
Total	$2,005,181,852	100.0%	$1,196,849,573	100.0%

n=206

 Loan funds account for most of the total amount originated.

The total dollar value of originations by purpose of loan or investment, and by type of CDFI is provided in Table 7-4. In this table, the data for the two loan funds that are outliers are not included. Even without the outliers, loan funds (the most numerous of the CDFIs) collectively originated $605 million of the nearly $1.2 billion in total originations. Banks originated nearly $409 million and credit unions originated just over $168 million.

There are some differences between types of CDFIs in terms of the purposes of the loans and equity investments originated. Loan funds focused almost half (46.4%) of their activity in housing development, especially the construction of new multi- and single-family housing. Loan funds concentrated nearly one-fifth (19.1%) of their activity in business development, for working capital and to a lesser extent the acquisition of fixed assets.

Banks and venture funds were primarily involved in business lending. Over a third (36.1%) of the value of bank originations, for instance, was for business. The comparable figure for venture funds was much higher. Over four out of every five dollars (83.6%) venture funds originated were for business development and expansion, with most of these monies supporting working capital. Unlike venture capital funds, banks originated a diverse range of loans, just over 19% of the total dollar value of bank originations supported residential real estate development. An equal amount – 13.5% – supported home purchase and improvement as well as *commercial real estate* development.

Table 7-4: Loans and Equity Investments Originated by Purpose and by Type of CDFI, Outliers Removed, FY 2003

	Banks	Credit Unions	Loan Funds	Venture Funds
Totals	**$408,993,152**	**$168,140,418**	**$604,977,416**	**$14,738,587**
Business – Fixed Asset	22.2%	6.8%	4.9%	13.8%
Business – Working Capital	13.8%	2.5%	14.2%	69.8%
Subtotal Business	**36.1%**	**9.3%**	**19.1%**	**83.6%**
Home Improvement	0.2%	1.7%	2.9%	0.0%
Home Purchase	13.2%	16.2%	10.7%	0.0%
Subtotal Home	**13.5%**	**17.9%**	**13.6%**	**0.0%**
Real Estate Construction, Commercial	12.8%	0.0%	5.6%	5.2%
Real Estate Rehabilitation, Commercial	0.7%	2.4%	3.1%	0.2%
Subtotal *Commercial Real Estate*	**13.5%**	**2.4%**	**8.7%**	**5.4%**
Real Estate Construction, Multi-Family	2.4%	0.0%	15.1%	0.0%
Real Estate Construction, Single Family	3.3%	2.2%	11.7%	0.0%
Real Estate Rehabilitation, Multi-Family	0.3%	0.0%	17.1%	0.0%
Real Estate Rehabilitation, Single Family	13.3%	0.0%	2.6%	0.0%
Residential Real Estate	19.4%	2.2%	46.4%	0.0%
Consumer	5.3%	55.5%	0.2%	0.0%
Other	12.4%	12.7%	11.9%	11.0%
Total	**100.0%**	**100.0%**	**100.0%**	**100.0%**

n=206

 The average bank originates significantly more loans and investments than any other type of CDFI.

When these same data are looked at in terms of the average amounts per CDFI, the picture changes. As shown in Table 7-5, analyzing the average per CDFI demonstrates that it is banks that by far originated the largest amount of loans and investments in FY 2003. The average bank originated $51.1 million, more than seven times any other type of CDFI. When the loan fund outliers are included, the average loan fund and credit union are comparable in originations: $6.6 million and $6.0 million, respectively. The average venture fund originated $2.1 million. When the loan fund outliers are removed, the average loan fund originated $3.7 million, placing it almost evenly between the average credit union and venture fund. See Table 7-6.

Table 7-5: Average Amount of Loans and Equity Investment Originated by Purpose and by Type of CDFI, FY 2003

	Banks	Credit Unions	Loan Funds	Venture Funds	All CDFIs
Business	$18,434,176	$557,429	$801,540	$1,759,798	$1,479,106
Home	$6,882,063	$1,076,045	$500,318	NA	$806,433
Commercial Real Estate	$6,878,056	$142,857	$431,604	$113,912	$629,983
Residential Real Estate	$9,919,229	$131,090	$4,385,641	NA	$3,878,149
Consumer	$2,688,852	$3,335,673	$7,581	NA	$558,464
Other	$6,321,767	$761,921	$516,758	$231,803	$763,441
Total	$51,124,145	$6,005,016	$6,643,443	$2,105,513	$8,115,578

n=208

Table 7-6: Average Amount of Loans and Equity Investment Originated by Purpose of Loan/Investment, Loan Funds Only, Outliers Removed, FY 2003

	Amount
Business	$709,969
Home	$506,457
Commercial Real Estate	$321,951
Residential Real Estate	$1,722,074
Consumer	$7,674
Other	$443,393
Total	$3,711,519

n=206

 Average loan and investment size varies by the purpose of the transaction and the type of financial institution.

Table 7-7 shows the average loan/investment amount by purpose and by institution type. As can be expected, real estate loans/investments tend to be the largest and consumer the smallest. Among the business lenders, venture funds and banks make significantly larger loans/investments than do loan funds and credit unions. In terms of commercial and residential real estate, loan funds make by far the largest loans, with averages above $400,000, compared to all other lenders whose averages are below $161,000. The large difference between loan fund and bank real estate loans must be qualified, however, because there are very few bank real estate loans in the sample: only one or two banks in the dataset originated residential construction, single family rehabilitation, and commercial rehabilitation loans in FY 2003.

Table 7-7: Average Size of Loans and Equity Investments Originated by CDFI Type, FY 2003

	Banks	Credit Unions	Loan Funds	Venture Funds
n	8	28	165	7
Business	$94,838	$26,680	$29,462	$143,239
Home	$40,965	$43,289	$25,621	NA
Commercial Real Estate	$125,914	$153,846	$406,941	$132,897
Residential Real Estate	$160,961	$49,602	$462,384	NA
Consumer	$6,312	$5,325	$1,017	NA
Other	$182,578	$37,626	$155,310	$202,828
Totals	$54,431	$8,628	$97,611	$147,386

 The vast majority of originations are term loans, even among venture funds.

CDFIs provide several different types of financing: term loans (including those with *equity-like features*), lines of credit, and equity investments. By far the most common type of transaction is the term loan. All of the other types of financing are far less common. Table 6-7 shows this breakdown by type of CDFI. The findings in Table 7-8 can be briefly summarized. Nearly 75% of the value of originations is in the form of term loans. However, term loans are more frequently used by credit unions (90.9%) and loan funds (81.1%) than either banks or venture funds. At one-third, equity investments represent a relatively large share of venture fund originations. Finally, lines of credit are comparatively important to banks in contrast to the other types of CDFIs.

With respect to venture capital funds, it should be noted that a large portion of their term loans may be debt with *equity-like features*. The terms of these loans include *equity-like features* that provide the lender some upside potential above the return of principal and interest. The feature can be tied either to future revenues (royalties) or to equity (convertible debt or debt with warrants), or may include an interest rate that adjusts based on the borrower's performance.

Table 7-8: Percent of the Value of Originations by Transaction Type and by Type of CDFI, Outliers Removed, FY 2003

	Banks	Credit Unions	Loan Funds	Venture Funds	All CDFIs
n	8	28	163	7	206
Term	54.3%	90.9%	81.8%	58.2%	73.4%
Line of Credit	12.5%	2.0%	7.8%	NA	8.5%
Equity	0.0%	0.7%	0.3%	33.2%	0.6%
Other	33.2%	6.4%	10.2%	8.6%	17.5%
Totals	100.0%	100.0%	100.0%	100.0%	100.0%

n=206

 Like other financial data, age of CDFI is directly related to the value of originations in FY 2003.

Originations, like data analyzed for portfolio outstanding or capital under management, are related to the age of the CDFI. The youngest CDFIs originated $82.3 million, CDFIs with between five and nine years of financing originated over double that, or $174.6 million, those institutions with 10 to 17 years experience originated $264.1 million, and those CDFIs with 18 or more years experience originated $676 million. See Figure 7-3.

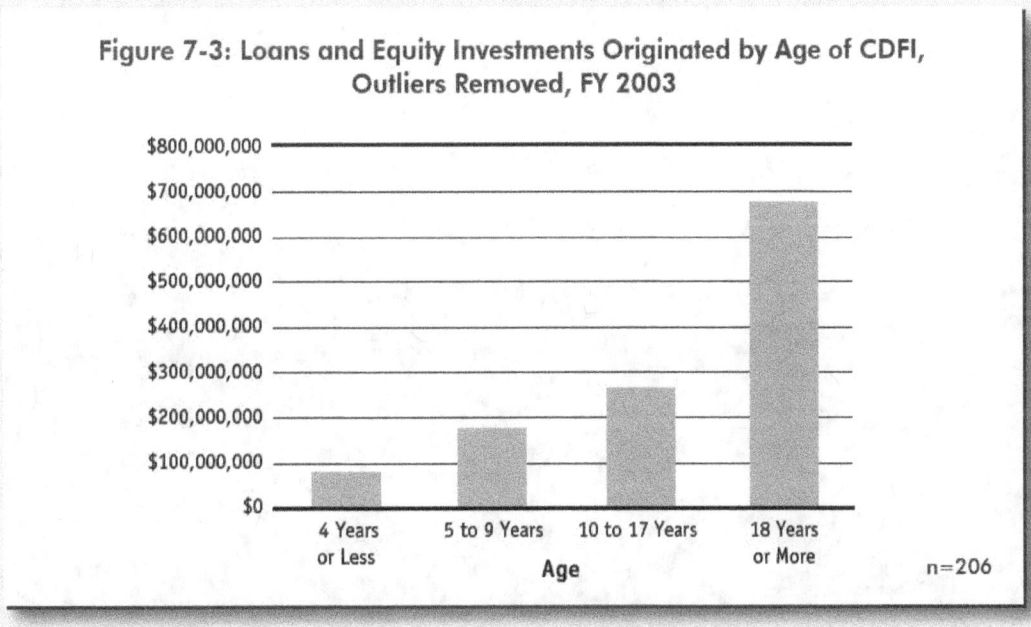

Figure 7-3: Loans and Equity Investments Originated by Age of CDFI, Outliers Removed, FY 2003

Note: This page left blank intentionally.

Loan Sales and Purchases

Few CDFIs report that they engaged in the sale or purchase of loans. Indeed, in FY 2003, 26 CDFIs (12%) reported that they sold 4,911 loans with a total presale book value of $524 million and 18 indicated that they purchased loans of more than $1 billion. These figures are skewed by a single CDFI, Self-Help, which accounts for more than half of loan sales and more than 97% of purchases. Nonetheless, because loan sales are a potential source of liquidity that more CDFIs may consider in the future, it is instructive to share the current sales activity reported in CIIS and to create a baseline from which to measure changes going forward. The end of the chapter presents a brief analysis on loan purchases.

 ## Selling loans on the *secondary market*

CDFIs are, for the most part, portfolio lenders. That is, CDFIs make loans to hold in portfolio rather than to sell. Portfolio lending has two advantages for CDFIs. First, it allows flexible underwriting so that CDFIs can tailor loans to meet the repayment abilities of different borrowers. Second, such lending provides CDFIs a predictable stream of interest payments over the term of the loan. There are, however, several disadvantages as well. Portfolio lending increases credit risk because CDFIs hold the risk of a borrower defaulting on a loan. Holding loans in portfolio also makes CDFIs subject to adverse interest rate movement: if a CDFI borrowed long-term capital when rates were high and is lending that capital when rates are low, it bears the loss associated with reduced interest rate spread. Finally, holding loans in portfolio limits liquidity: if a CDFI lends out its entire capital pool, its ability to make new loans is limited by the volume and schedule of repayments it receives. Unless it makes short-term loans, it may take some time for loan payments to accumulate.

Selling loans can offset these disadvantages. Selling loans transfers the risk of borrower default to others (unless they are sold with the provision that the seller must replace non-performing loans, a condition known as "recourse"). CDFIs that sell loans are not as adversely affected by interest rate fluctuations because they are less dependent on borrowed capital to capitalize their loan pool. Finally, loan sales generate liquidity, continually providing CDFIs with a source of capital to make new loans.

▶ **CDFIs sold $524 million in loans in FY 2003.**

Twenty-six CDFIs reported selling loans with a pre-sale book value of $524 million. Table 8-1 shows which types of CDFIs sold loans. Half of the reporting banks sold loans. A significantly smaller percentage of credit unions (14%) and loan funds (10%) sold loans. None of the reporting venture funds sold loans. In terms of dollar amounts, loan funds accounted for nearly 90% of the pre-sale book value of the loans sold. Banks accounted for almost 6% and credit unions almost 5%.

Table 8-1: Loan Sales by Type of CDFI, FY 2003

	CDFIs	CDFIs that Sold Loans		Pre-Sale Book Value of Loans Sold	
	Number	Number	Percent	Amount	Percent
Banks	8	4	50.0%	$29,272,644	5.6%
Credit Unions	28	4	14.3%	$23,695,575	4.5%
Loan Funds	178	18	10.1%	$471,333,239	89.9%
Venture Funds	9	0	0.0%	$0	0.0%
Total	223	26	11.7%	$524,301,458	100.0%

As noted above, Self-Help, one of the oldest and largest CDFIs, sold more than half of all loans sold. Self-Help's sales account for $277 million of the $471 million sold by all loan funds. Self-Help's sales were primarily mortgage loans ($264 million), with a relatively small amount of business loans ($13 million). As shown in Table 8-2, when Self-Help is removed, loan funds still account for the vast majority of loans sold (78.6%), while banks and credit unions each count for approximately one-tenth. For the remainder of this chapter, Self-Help is removed except where noted.

Table 8-2: Loan Sales by Type of CDFI, Outlier Removed, FY 2003

	CDFIs	CDFIs that Sold Loans		Pre-Sale Book Value of Loans Sold	
	Number	Number	Percent	Amount	Percent
Banks	8	4	50.0%	$29,272,644	11.9%
Credit Unions	28	4	14.3%	$23,695,575	9.6%
Loan Funds	177	17	9.6%	$194,164,198	78.6%
Venture Funds	9	0	0.0%	$0	0.0%
Total	222	25	12.2%	$246,968,219	100.0%

As Table 8-3 shows, even when Self-Help is removed, CDFI loan sales are dominated by mortgage loans. Four-fifths (79.3%) of the pre-sale book value of loans sold were mortgage loans. Nearly all loans sold by credit unions were mortgages (99.95%) and nearly 90% of loans sold by loan funds were mortgages. Banks, in contrast, sold primarily business loans (44.5%) and other loans (47.5%).

Table 8-3: Pre-Sale Book Value of Loans Sold by Type of CDFI, Outlier Removed, FY 2003

	Business	Mortgage	Commercial Real Estate	Other Loans	All Sold Loans
n	5	17	3	5	25
Banks	$13,039,979	$574,820	$1,750,080	$13,907,765	$29,272,644
Credit Unions	$0	$23,684,767	$0	$10,808	$23,695,575
Loan Funds	$2,407,703	$171,697,367	$14,012,715	$5,882,215	$194,000,000
Total	$15,447,682	$195,956,954	$15,762,795	$19,800,788	$246,968,219
Banks	44.5%	2.0%	6.0%	47.5%	100.0%
Credit Unions	0.0%	99.95%	0.0%	0.046%	100.0%
Loan Funds	1.2%	88.5%	7.2%	3.0%	100.0%
Total	6.3%	79.3%	6.4%	8.0%	100.0%

 Large CDFIs account for the vast majority of loan sales.

As Table 8-4 demonstrates, the largest CDFIs – those with $15 million or more in assets – are responsible for selling nearly all (96.8%) of the CDFI loans sold. This holds true across all types of CDFIs.

Table 8-4: Percent of Pre-Sale Book Value of Total Loans Sold by Type of CDFI and Size of CDFI, Outlier Removed, FY 2003

	Less than $1.5 Million	$1.5 to $4.9 Million	$5.0 to $14.9 Million	$15.0 Million or more	All CDFIs
n	0	1	5	19	25
Banks	NA[1]	NA	NA	100.0%	100%
Credit Unions	NA	NA	2.9%	97.1%	100%
Loan Funds	NA	0.2%	4.0%	95.8%	100%
Total	NA	0.1%	3.1%	96.8%	100%

 Older CDFIs are more active in selling loans than younger CDFIs, but young banks are also active sellers.

Looking at age, Table 8-5 shows that the relationship between age of CDFI and loan sales is not as clearly defined as the relationship between size and sales. While among loan funds the oldest institutions do 72.2% of the selling, among regulated institutions sales are more evenly spread across age categories. Credit unions that are 10-17 years old accounted for almost as much in loan sales as credit unions aged 18 or more years (46.9% and 53.1%, respectively.) Banks that were five to nine years old were responsible for more sales than banks that were 18 years old or more. The differences between regulated and

---

[1]NA indicates that there are no reporting CDFIs that meet this criterion.

non-regulated CDFIs in sales by age may be explained by the fact that the regulated financial institution industry is an active *secondary market* participant and views selling loans is a normal course of business. Among the relatively young non-regulated CDFI industry, selling loans is not yet a normal course of business. Younger CDFIs tend to be able to satisfy their capital needs through grants and borrowed capital. They are unfamiliar with the *secondary market*, and do not have a need to tap into it. Older CDFIs, on the other hand, have larger capital needs which cannot always be satisfied by raising more grants or borrowing more funds. They have to consider other options such as selling loans to meet their growing needs.

Table 8-5: Percent of Pre-Sale Book Value of Total Loans Sold by Type of CDFI and Age of CDFI, Outlier Removed, FY 2003

	1 to 4 Years	5 to 9 Years	10 to 17 Years	18 Years or More	All CDFIs
n	2	4	9	10	25
Banks	14.6%	37.5%	12.0%	35.9%	100%
Credit Unions	NA	NA	46.9%	53.1%	100%
Loan Funds	0.2%	9.6%	18.1%	72.2%	100%
Total	2.9%	13.4%	21.4%	62.3%	100%

 The purchasers of CDFI loans

FY 2003 was the first year the Fund attempted to identify the purchasers of CDFI loans. The Fund allowed CDFIs, when reporting data, to choose from five well-known loan purchasers: the Community Reinvestment Fund (CRF), Fannie Mae, Freddie Mac, Neighborhood Housing Services of America (NHSA)[2], and the Small Business Administration (SBA). A sixth option, Other, captured all other purchasers. When Self-Help was included in the analysis, Fannie Mae accounted for more than half (57%) of the purchases (measured in pre-sale book value). When Self-Help is excluded, Other accounts for more than half (58%). As Figure 8-1 shows, Freddie Mac is the second largest purchaser with nearly one-quarter (23%) of purchases. Fannie Mae is third with 13%. NHSA, CRF, and the SBA each purchased 3% or less.

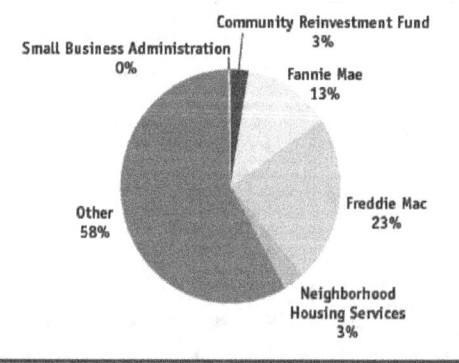

Figure 8-1: Pre-Sale Book Value of Loans by Loan Purchaser, Outlier Excluded, FY 2003

Small Business Administration 0%
Community Reinvestment Fund 3%
Fannie Mae 13%
Freddie Mac 23%
Neighborhood Housing Services 3%
Other 58%

---

[2] Neighborhood Housing Services of America (NHSA) purchases loans from the national NeighborWorks® network of 230 nonprofit NeighborWorks® organizations. A number of NeighborWorks® organizations are certified CDFIs.

These results raise the question: which entities are included in Other? Follow-up interviews with 12 CDFIs provided the answer. Seven of the 12 CDFIs sold all or part of their loans to local, regional and national banks. In fact, at least 75% of the 12 CDFIs' other sales went to banks.[3] The second largest other purchaser was housing finance authorities. Three CDFIs sold to housing finance authorities, but these sales represented only about 7% of other sales, a distant second to banks. Two CDFIs sold to investment banks. Five other purchasers were each mentioned by a single CDFI: Federal Agricultural Mortgage Corporation (Farmer Mac), the United State Department of Agriculture's (USDA) Farm Services, a mortgage company, a pool of insurance companies, and a utility company. In conclusion, a wide range of entities purchased CDFI loans. The next section examines the pricing the various purchasers provided.

 Most loans were sold at par.

Table 8-6 provides some of the details of these loan sales. For each purchaser, the table shows total annual sales to that purchaser, the number of CDFIs that sold to that purchaser, and the number of those CDFIs that received par, a premium or a discount on their total annual sales to that purchaser. Self-Help's sales are included in this analysis.

Table 8-6: Loan Sales by Purchaser and Price, FY 2003

| | Total Loan Sales | | Number of CDFIs Selling[4] | Number of CDFIs Selling at | | |
	Amount	Number		Par	Premium	Discount
CRF	$6,828,365	23	3	3	0	0
Fannie Mae	$294,049,151	3,344	7	5	1	1
Freddie Mac	$54,838,980	19	1	1	0	0
NHSA	$7,202,053	236	6	6	0	0
SBA	$22,599,045	59	2	0	2	0
Other	$139,395,255	1,230	16	12	3	1
Total	$524,912,849	4,911	NA	NA	NA	NA

Par means the sale price equals the pre-sale book value of the loans sold. Premium means the sale price exceeds the pre-sale book value and discount means the sale price is less than the pre-sale book value. As the table shows, most sales were at par. Only three purchasers paid premiums and only two paid discounts. Fannie Mae paid a premium to only one of the seven CDFIs that sold to it during FY 2006. SBA paid premiums to the two CDFIs that sold loans to it. Other purchasers paid premiums to only three of the 16 CDFIs that sold to it during the year. Fannie Mae paid a discount to one of the seven CDFI sellers and other purchasers paid a discount to only one of their 16 CDFI sellers.

---

[3] Not all the CDFIs that sold to more than one purchaser provided a breakdown of sales to each entity. Factoring in the missing date, it is clear that more than 75% of loans were sold to banks.

[4] The total number of CDFIs selling does not add up to 26 because some CDFIs sold to more than one purchaser.

Table 8-7 summarizes the value of the discounts and premiums CDFIs received for their loans. It is important to note that CDFIs reported their aggregate sales to a particular purchaser during the year. So, if a CDFI sold three pools of loans to one purchaser at different times throughout the year, all of these sales would have been reported as a single sale. From these data the Fund was able to calculate the discount or premium that each purchaser provided to each seller for the year's total sales.

Table 8-7: Loan Sale Premiums and Discounts by Purchaser, FY 2003

Purchaser	Premium / Discount	Number of CDFIs that Sold at a Premium or Discount	Premiums and (Discounts)		
			Average	High	Low
Fannie Mae	Premium	1	2.13%	2.13%	2.13%
	Discount	1	(1.17%)	(1.17%)	(1.17%)
Other	Premium	3	3.60%	7.78%	1.42%
	Discount	1	(0.10%)	(0.10%)	(0.10%)
SBA	Premium	2	2.14%	2.28%	2.00%

As the above table shows, premiums ranged from a high of 7.78% to a low of 1.42%, both paid by other purchasers. Discounts were more modest, ranging from .10% to 1.17%. For sales to the SBA, the Fund also analyzed how many of the loans or portions of loans sold were guaranteed. The CDFI that received the 2.28% premium sold mostly guaranteed loans to SBA: 70.0% of the pre-sale value of the loans sold was guaranteed. None of the loans sold for the 2.14% premium were guaranteed.

 Eighteen CDFIs purchased loans in FY 2003.

As stated above, a very small number of CDFIs reported purchasing more than $1 billion in loans in FY 2003. Self-Help alone was responsible for all but $39 million of these purchases under its mortgage purchase program.

While the numbers are small when Self-Help is excluded, it is interesting to note that all types of CDFIs except venture funds purchased loans and that they purchased a variety of types of loans. All of the eight banks in the sample purchased loans. These institutions were responsible for 60% of the purchases, buying mortgage, business, *commercial real estate* and other loans. Eight loan funds purchased nearly 30% of the loans, nearly all (96%) of which were mortgages. Credit unions purchased the remaining loans (11.3%), nearly all of which were mortgages followed by other types of loans. Tables 8-8 and 8-9 show these figures.

Table 8-8: CDFI Loan Purchases by Type of CDFI, Outlier Excluded, FY 2003

	Number of CDFIs	Total Purchases	Percent of Total Purchases
Banks	5	$23,346,281	59.2%
Credit Unions	4	$4,441,917	11.3%
Loan Funds	8	$11,632,297	29.5%
Venture Funds	0	$0	0.0%
Total	17	$39,420,4951	100.0%

Table 8-9: Loans Purchased by Purpose and by Type of CDFI, Outlier Removed, FY 2003

	Business	Mortgage	Commercial Real Estate	Other	All CDFIs
n	4	8	2	4	17
Total Amount	$6,570,147	$21,632,955	$5,109,739	$6,107,654	$39,420,495
Banks	27.4%	31.5%	21.9%	19.2%	100.0%
Credit Unions	2.0%	70.4%	0.0%	27.6%	100.0%
Loan Funds	0.7%	95.9%	0.0%	3.4%	100.0%
Total	16.7%	54.9%	13.0%	15.5%	100.0%

Finally, while CDFIs of all ages purchased loans, nearly all purchasers were large in terms of assets. See tables 8-10 and 8-11.

Table 8-10 Loans Purchased by Age of CDFI, Outlier Excluded, FY 2003

	1 to 4 Years	5 to 9 Years	10 to 17 Years	18 Years or More	All CDFIs
n	5	2	5	5	17
Total	$11,238,830	$7,344,876	$17,813,234	$3,023,555	$39,420,495
Percent	28.5%	18.6%	45.2%	7.7%	100.0%

Table 8-11 Loans Purchased by Size of CDFI, Outlier Excluded, FY 2003

	Less than $1.5 Million	$1.5 to $4.9 Million	$5.0 to $14.9 Million	$15.0 Million or more	All CDFIs
n	1	3	3	10	17
Total	$11,214	$1,112,580	$4,183,758	$34,112,943	$39,420,495
Percent[5]	0.03%	2.82%	10.61%	86.54%	100.00%

---

[5] The percentages do not add up to 100.0% due to rounding.

Note: This page left blank intentionally.

Financial Strength of CDFIs

There are many reasons to expect that CDFIs would be susceptible to financial problems. For one, CDFIs target their financial products and services to economically distressed communities in both urban and rural areas that have experienced high levels of unemployment and diminished investment. Another is that CDFIs serve populations which may have no or little experience with traditional financial service providers.

Contrary to expectations, however, our analysis shows that CDFIs are for the most part viable and strong financial institutions. While many CDFIs have been providing financing for only a few years and most are quite modest in terms of asset size, on the whole they have served distressed areas and populations while maintaining an admirable level of financial health.

The analysis shows that there is frequently a relationship between the age and size of a CDFI and positive outcomes on the financial ratios. CDFIs that have been providing financing for 10 or 20 years and have substantially more assets are especially strong in terms of financial measures. They are least dependent upon grants and philanthropic resources and have the lowest portfolio at risk and experience the lowest levels of loan losses. These relationships hold true even when banks, the majority of the oldest CDFIs, are removed from the analysis.

While CDFIs that have only a few years of financing experience and that are small institutions did not fare quite as well, for the most part they are financially healthy. Smaller and younger CDFIs, for example, deployed their available capital at comparable rates as the larger more mature CDFIs. These institutions also had sufficient resources to meet present operating needs, had a relatively small proportion of their total portfolio delinquent, and suffered only low levels of loan losses.

 Self-Sufficiency Rate

The self-sufficiency rate measures the extent to which an organization is covering its operating expenses through earned income rather than through grants or other contributions. A self-sufficiency rate of 100% indicates that a CDFI has earned exactly enough income to cover expenses in a particular fiscal year. The self-sufficiency rate is calculated by this formula:

Self-sufficiency Rate = Total Earned Income/Total Expenses

The plot of the average self-sufficiency rates by age and size groups of CDFIs is shown in Figure 9-1. Overall, the self-sufficiency rates for CIIS respondents vary from 0% to 250%, with a mean of 56% and a median of 47%.

Figure 9-1: Average Self-Sufficiency Rate by Age and Size of CDFI, FY 2003

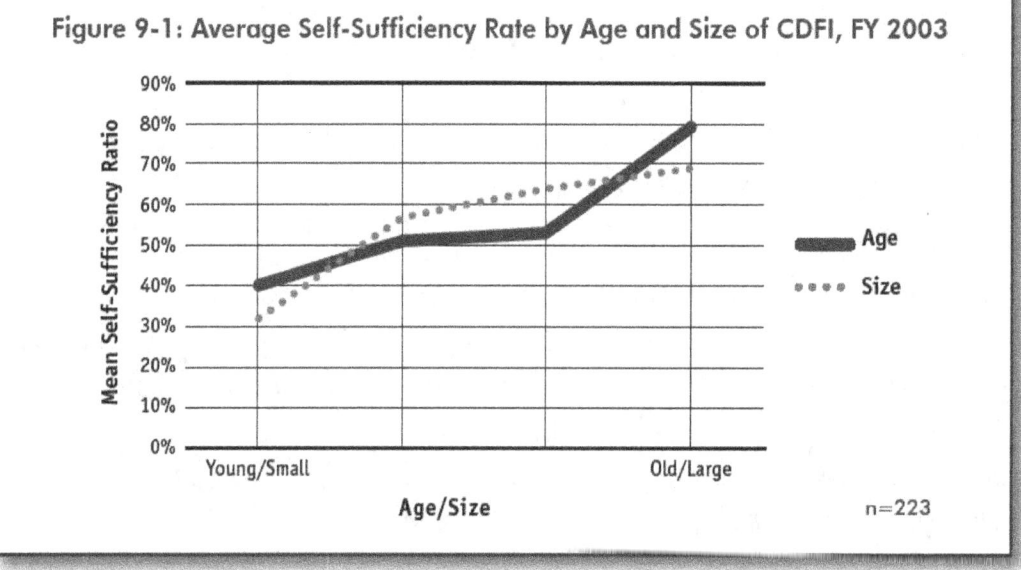

It is clear that there is a relationship both between age and size of CDFI and the self-sufficiency rate. Consistently, the youngest and smallest CDFIs have the lowest self-sufficiency rates and the older and largest CDFIs have the highest self-sufficiency rates. As CDFIs mature and evolve into larger financial institutions, they are more able to cover their operating expenses with income earned from loan portfolios, fees, and services rather than having to rely upon grants or other sources of unearned income. This relationship holds true even when regulated institutions are removed from the analysis.

Table 9-1 provides self-sufficiency rates by type and age of CDFI. These data are also broken out for regulated and unregulated institutions, and for-profit and non-profit institutions. While the self-sufficiency rate for each type of CDFI trends upward with age, these data show how self-sufficiency levels differ across types of CDFIs, and particularly between regulated and non-regulated CDFIs, and for-profit and non-profit CDFIs. The self-sufficiency rate is consistently higher for regulated and for-profit CDFIs, and lower for unregulated and non-profit institutions.

Table 9-1: Self-Sufficiency Rates by Type and Age of CDFI, FY 2003[1]

	4 Years or Less	5 to 9 Years	10 to 17 Years	18 Years or More	All CDFIs
n	59	50	55	59	223
Banks	54%	103%	124%	118%	110%
Credit Unions	55%	85%	86%	108%	97%
Loan Funds	38%	45%	49%	59%	47%
Venture Funds	47%	78%	*	*	59%
Regulated	55%	91%	101%	110%	99%
Unregulated	39%	49%	49%	59%	48%
For-Profit	50%	106%	89%	118%	88%
Non-Profit	39%	46%	50%	76%	53%
Total	40%	51%	53%	79%	56%

These same rates are provided by size and type of CDFI in Table 9-2. Again, it is clear that regulated and for-profit CDFIs consistently have higher self-sufficiency rates than their unregulated and non-profit counterparts with similarly sized total assets.

Table 9-2: Self-Sufficiency Rates by Type and Size of CDFI, FY 2003[2]

	$1.5 Million or Less	$1.5 to $4.9 Million	$5.0 to $14.9 Million	$15.0 Million or more
n	52	58	54	59
Banks	NA	NA	NA	110%
Credit Unions	90%	78%	103%	113%
Loan Funds	29%	51%	53%	58%
Venture Funds	26%	*	*	57%
Regulated	90%	78%	103%	111%
Unregulated	29%	53%	52%	58%
For-Profit	28%[3]	101%	NA	100%
Non-Profit	33%	54%	52%	62%
Total	32%	57%	64%	69%

[1] When there are two or fewer venture funds or loan funds reporting, the data is suppressed. This rule does not apply to banks and credit unions because their individual financial data is publicly available.

[2] An asterisk indicates that data has been suppressed due to insufficient observations.

[3] Three CDFIs are included in this response. The total assets of these three CDFIs average less than $200,000 each.

▶ Deployment Ratio

The deployment ratio indicates the extent to which an organization's capital under management is actually deployed in loans or equity investments. This ratio serves as an indicator of how aggressively an organization has used its capital. A high deployment ratio is an indication that a CDFI is using its most valuable resource, its loan and investment capital, productively. A deployment ratio of 1.0 indicates that a CDFI has fully deployed all available capital under management.[4] The formula to calculate this ratio is:

Deployment Ratio = Total Loan and Investment Portfolio Outstanding/ Total Capital under Management

Figure 9-2 shows the relationship between both age and size of CDFI and the deployment ratio. This shows that while the deployment ratio is higher for older and larger CDFIs, there are in fact only modest differences in this measure between the youngest and smallest CDFIs and the older, larger CDFIs. In FY 2003, the deployment ratio for the CDFIs providing these data averaged .67 with a median of .69. Fewer than 20% of the CDFIs providing data for FY 2003 had deployment ratios of .50 or less.

Even more so than the self-sufficiency rate, there is a very close relationship between age and size of CDFI and the deployment ratio. Even though the differences are very small, younger and smaller CDFIs

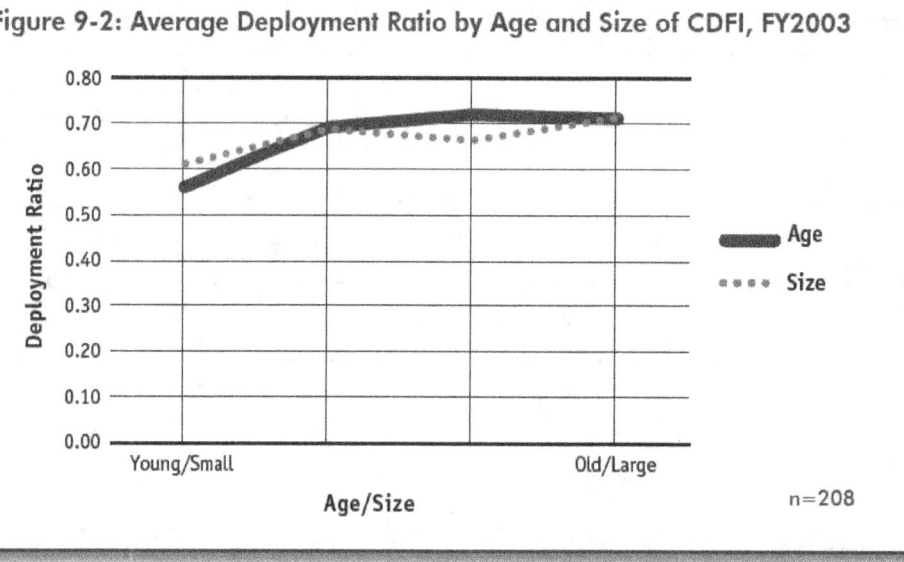

Figure 9-2: Average Deployment Ratio by Age and Size of CDFI, FY2003

---

[4]The definition of capital under management does not take into consideration off-balance sheet capital or capital that has been committed to a borrower or investee but not yet originated.

are somewhat less effective in fully using their resources as income-producing loans; older and larger CDFIs are somewhat more aggressive in using their resources. These findings are not surprising. While a young CDFI may be able to obtain lending and investing capital relatively quickly, it may not be able to put this capital to immediate use because of the time needed to develop underwriting and loan monitoring policies, market its products, underwrite its first loans and build a portfolio.

 Operating Liquidity Ratio

The operating liquidity ratio is a measure of the extent to which an organization has sufficient operating reserves on hand to pay its expenses. A ratio of 1.0 or greater indicates that an organization has enough liquid assets on hand to cover three months of expenses. A ratio of less than 1.0 indicates that an organization may be experiencing operating liquidity problems. The formula for the operating liquidity ratio is:

Operating Liquidity Ratio = Total Unrestricted Cash and Cash Equivalents/ (Pre-Tax Expenses * .25)

The mean operating liquidity ratio in FY 2003 was 6.8 and the median was 3.5. Figure 9-3 shows these ratios by age and size of CDFI. The ratios shown in the figure range from 3.89 to 9.01, indicating that CDFIs in each group, on average, have strong liquidity. However, what the figure does not show is that 41 (18.4%) CDFIs had an operating liquidity ratio of less than 1.0 and may, therefore, not have sufficient liquid assets to deal with intermittent demands for cash.

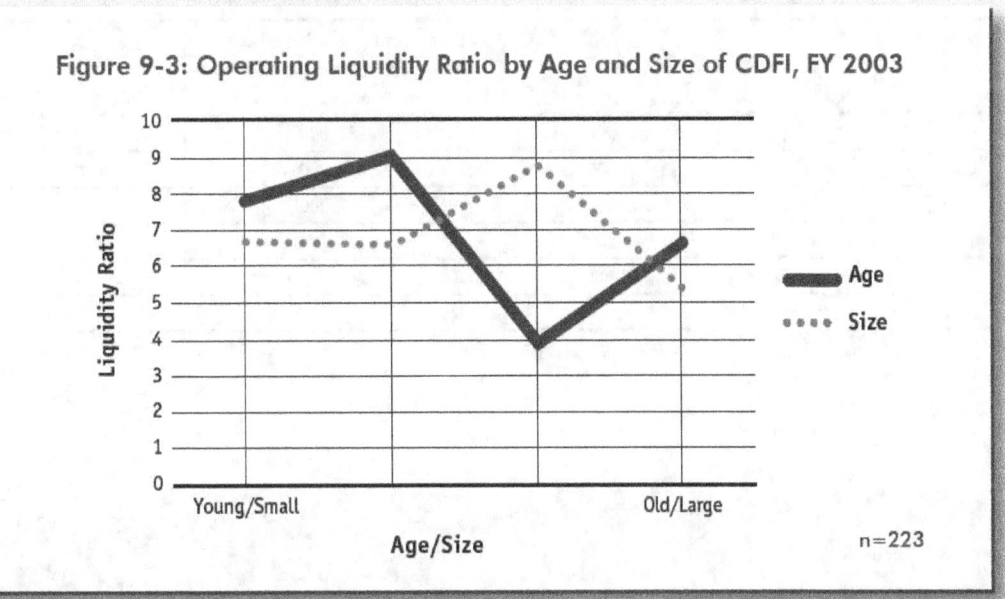

Figure 9-3: Operating Liquidity Ratio by Age and Size of CDFI, FY 2003

Portfolio at Risk

Portfolio at risk measures the proportion of loans that are 90 days or more past due and likely to end up in default. This ratio, like the loan loss ratio, is important because it is a predictor of the likely future economic health of the institution. The formula for this ratio for all CDFIs except credit unions is:

Portfolio at Risk = Total Balance Outstanding of Loans with Payments that are 90 Days or More Past Due/Total Outstanding Loan Portfolio

For credit unions, the formula is:

Portfolio at Risk (Credit Unions) = Total Balance Outstanding of Loans with Payments that are 60 days or More Past Due/Total Outstanding Loan Portfolio

Portfolio at risk (as well as the loan loss ratio and loan loss reserve ratio, the two other portfolio quality indicators included in this report) can be measured in two ways. First, the portfolio at risk for the combined portfolio of each group analyzed. Second, the average portfolio at risk for the CDFIs in each group. To illustrate the difference, Table 9-3 shows that a group of three CDFIs may have a combined portfolio at risk of 2% but an average portfolio at risk of 5%. The difference is that in the combined portfolio calculation, the low portfolio at risk rates of the CDFIs with the large portfolios overshadow the high portfolio at risk rate of the CDFI with the small portfolio. In the average portfolio calculation, all portfolio at risk rates are treated equally regardless of the size of the portfolio.

Table 9-3: Sample Portfolio at Risk Calculations

	Outstanding Loan Portfolio	Balance Outstanding of Loans with Payments that are 90 Days or More Past Due	Portfolio at Risk
CDFI A	$1,000,000	$30,000	3%
CDFI B	$5,000,000	$50,000	1%
CDFI C	$300,000	$30,000	10%
Total	$6,300,000	$110,000	
Portfolio at Risk of Combined Portfolio = $6,300,000 / $110,000			2%
Average Portfolio at Risk = (3%+1%+10%)/3			5%

In this chapter, the portfolio quality analysis is based on average portfolios. This approach is consistent with the other analyses in this report and is intended to show the performance of the average CDFI in each group being analyzed. It should be noted that the average portfolio rates for the CIIS respondents, like the three CDFIs in the example above, are higher than the combined portfolio rates: the average portfolio at risk is 4.43% versus a combined rate of 2.5%, while the average loan loss rate is 2.2% versus a combined loss rate of less than one percent (.7%). For comparison purposes, the portfolio quality analysis based on combined portfolios is provided in Appendix F.[5]

Table 9-4 provides the average portfolio at risk rates by type and age of CDFI. As can be seen in the table, average portfolio at risk is very small for all types of CDFIs across age groups.

Table 9-4: Average Portfolio at Risk by Age and Type of CDFI, FY 2003[6]

	4 Years or Less	5 to 9 Years	10 to 17 Years	18 Years or More	All CDFIs
n	57	50	52	57	213[7]
Banks	*	*	*	1.20%	1.46%
Credit Unions	2.01%	*	4.25%	2.90%	2.94%
Loan Funds	2.45%	6.34%	5.15%	6.27%	4.88%
Venture Funds	1.06%	7.06%	*	*	3.22%
Total	2.33%	6.14%	4.79%	4.79%	4.43%

The average portfolio at risk for all CDFIs in FY 2003 was 4.43%. In fact, nearly a third (32.7%) of CDFIs reported no loans at risk; however 19.2% of CDFIs reported at risk rates exceeding 6.0%, 13.1% reported 10.0% or higher and 6.5% of the CDFIs in FY 2003 reported at risk ratios of 20% or higher.

A plot of the average portfolio at risk by size and age of CDFI is shown in Figure 9-4. Both age and size of CDFI are related to the average at risk rate in similar ways: the at risk rate is lowest for younger and smaller CDFIs, increases for somewhat older and larger CDFIs, but decreases for the oldest and largest CDFIs.

---

[5] The CDFI Data Project (CDP) bases its portfolio quality analysis on combined portfolios. To compare the performance of CDFIs in the CDP dataset to CDFIs in the CIIS dataset, one must use the combined portfolio analysis in Appendix F.

[6] An asterisk indicates that data has been suppressed due to insufficient observations.

[7] The data for 10 CDFIs are not included in the table. Seven of these did not provide portfolio data. The other three reported zero financing outstanding because one had not begun financing activities, another made no loans due to lack of funding, and another originated loans on its parent's books.

Figure 9-4: Average Portfolio at Risk by Age and Size of CDFI, FY 2003

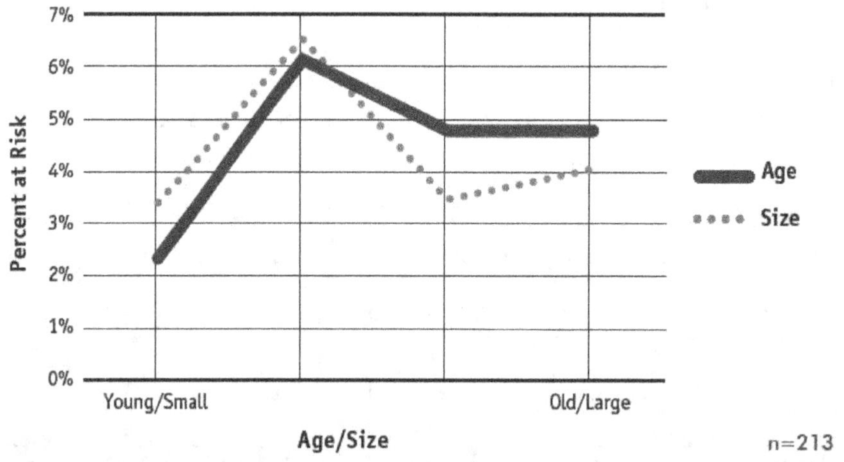

n=213

Loan Loss Ratio

The annual net loan loss ratio represents the portion of an organization's loan portfolio that has been deemed uncollectible and assumed to be a loss. The formula is:

Loan Loss Ratio = Net Amount Charged Off/Total Loans Outstanding

Different CDFIs have different policies on the circumstances under which they will charge off non-performing loans. While some CDFIs may establish a 90 day charge-off policy, others may not charge off until 120 days or longer. Given the variation in charge-off policies, a comparison of charge-off rates among CDFIs does not provide truly comparable data, except across regulated CDFIs. Even so, an examination of charge-off experiences is informative.

In FY 2003, the average loan loss ratio was 2.2%, with nearly half (48.0%) of all CDFIs reporting no losses at all. A plot of average loan losses by age and size of CDFI is shown in Figure 9-5.

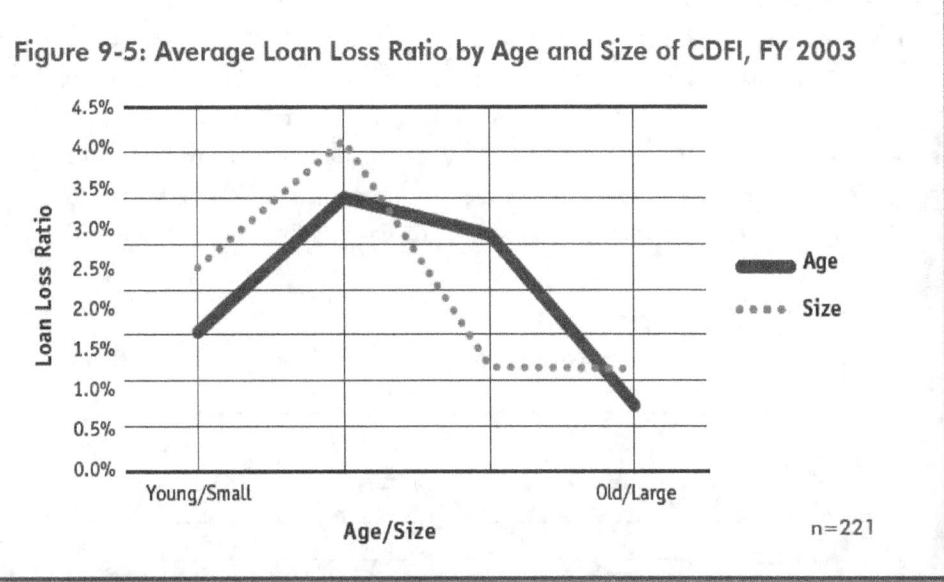

Figure 9-5: Average Loan Loss Ratio by Age and Size of CDFI, FY 2003

Average loan loss rates are lowest for both the least and most experienced CDFIs (2.0% and 1.2%, respectively). The CDFIs that have been financing between 5 and 10 years had the highest loan loss rate (3.5%), but this rate, as can be seen on the graph, then steadily declines. This pattern may be explained by the fact that less experienced institutions tend not to charge off loans early on, either because they are not making risky loans, loans with long maturity periods have not had time to become delinquent, or they do not have a charge off policy in place. As institutions mature, they tend to make riskier loans, loans with longer maturity dates may experience payment problems, and the institutions develop policies and procedures for charge offs.

 Loan Loss Reserve Ratio

CDFIs, like all financial institutions, keep some of their resources in reserve to cover loan losses. These are called loan loss reserves. To compare such reserves across different financial institutions, or by different sectors of the CDFI industry, the loan loss reserve is expressed as a proportion of the total loan portfolio outstanding. The formula for this ratio is:

Loan Loss Reserve Ratio = Loan Loss Reserve/Total Outstanding Loan Portfolio

Loan loss reserves may be either accrual reserves or cash reserves. Typically, accrual reserves are much larger than the cash reserves set aside to deal with losses from bad loans.

The average loan loss reserve ratios by age and size of CDFI are plotted in Figure 9-6. The ratios shown here are based on total loss reserves. In FY 2003, the average loan loss reserve ratio was 12.1% with a median of 7.0%. Loan loss reserves should be adequate to cover historical losses, presuming that historical losses are fair predictors of future losses. A comparison of Figures 9-5 and 9-6 shows that although reserves do not follow the same pattern as losses, they are in fact adequate to cover expected losses: for all age and size categories, reserves are at least 84.7% higher than losses. Indeed, in FY03, about 4 out of 5 (81.6%) of the CDFIs reporting held reserves that were adequate to cover their historical losses.

Figure 9-6: Average Loan Loss Reserve Ratio by Age and Size of CDFI, FY 2003

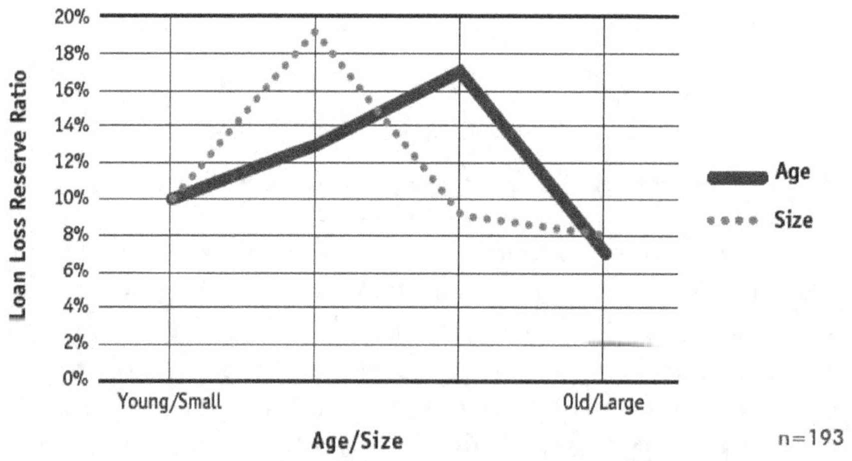

▶ **Average Net Revenue**

The Fund asks CIIS respondents to provide total revenue and expense information not only for the present fiscal year, but for 2 previous years as well. From these data, the average net revenue (total revenues less total expenses) is calculated from all three years:

Average Net Revenue = (Sum of Total Revenue in Current and 2 Previous Years) - (Sum of Total Expenses in Current and 2 Previous Years)

Average net revenue is a measure of financial health that takes into account the uneven revenue flow that some CDFIs experience due to multi-year operating grants or large investment capital grants. A CDFI that receives a grant that will cover a portion of the current and next year's operating costs may show large net revenue in the year the grant is received and negative net revenue the following year. In this case, the negative net revenue is not a sign of financial weakness because the CDFI received revenue last year to cover this year's expenses. The three-year average evens out the revenue stream and is a more accurate picture of financial health.

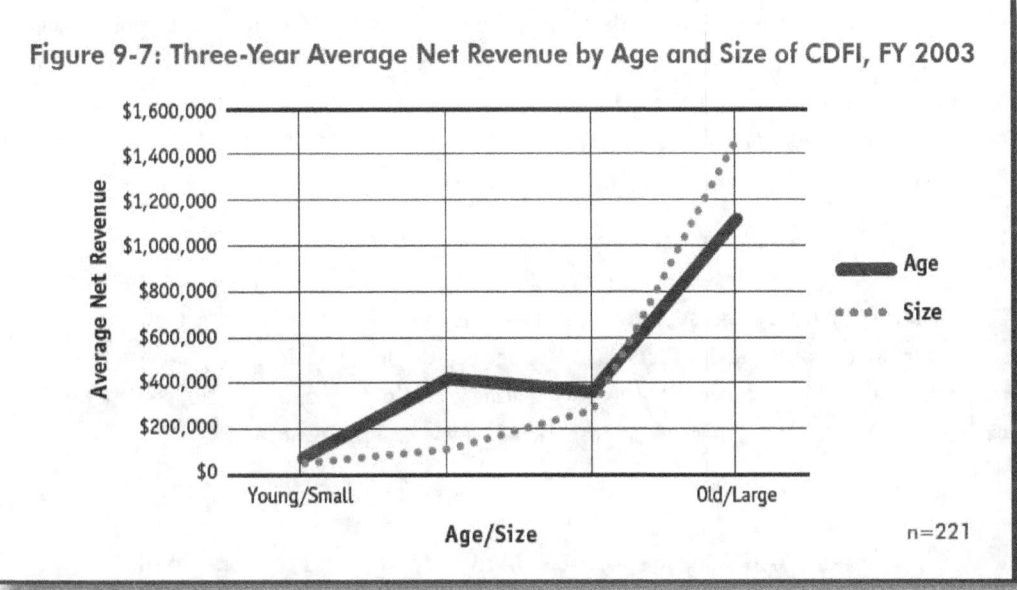

Figure 9-7: Three-Year Average Net Revenue by Age and Size of CDFI, FY 2003

The data in Figure 9-7 show that there is a very strong and linear relationship between size of CDFI and average net revenue. Average net revenue is modest with the smallest and youngest CDFIs and increases in steps over time and as CDFIs' total assets increase. Then, with the very largest and oldest CDFIs, the average net revenue increases dramatically.

▶ Net Asset Ratio

The net asset ratio serves as an indicator of the underlying financial strength of an organization and its ability to cover unexpected losses. The formula for this ratio is:

Net Asset Ratio = Net Assets / Total Assets

Regulated financial institutions are required by their regulators to maintain net asset ratios in the range of 7% to 9%. The Fund generally expects its unregulated CDFI awardees to maintain a net asset ratio of 20% or more. Figure 9-8 shows the mean net asset ratio by age and size for all regulated and non-regulated CDFIs. On average, regulated CDFIs maintain net asset ratios between 5.4% and 14.0%. Non-regulated CDFIs, whether due to restrictions imposed by funders and investors or other reasons, maintain net asset ratios ranging from 31.4% for the youngest CDFIs to nearly 48.0% for more mature CDFIs and coming down to below 45% for the oldest CDFIs.

These results can be interpreted in two ways. On one hand, non-regulated CDFIs should be able to withstand large unforeseen losses and remain financially viable. On the other hand, non-regulated CDFIs' relatively high net asset ratios may be unduly limiting their provision of community development services: rather than using their net assets to leverage additional debt capital, they are managing smaller portfolios that create less community impact. The management of the net asset ratio is a delicate balance that requires trade offs between financial health and community impact.

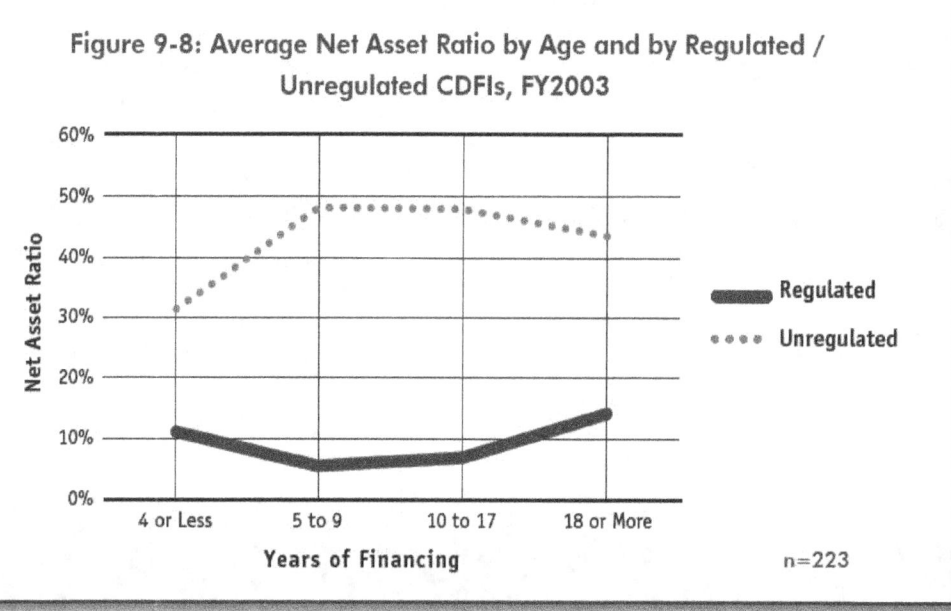

Figure 9-8: Average Net Asset Ratio by Age and by Regulated / Unregulated CDFIs, FY2003

Benefits to the Community

*CDFIs bring many benefits to the communities in which they invest. Some benefits, such as the number of new **affordable housing** units built or the number of jobs created by a new business, are relatively easy for CDFIs to measure. Others, such as the difference a new childcare center makes for low-income children and their parents, or the difference credit counseling makes to a struggling household, are more complicated and difficult to measure. CIIS allows CDFIs to report on some of the easily quantifiable benefits. In addition to **affordable housing** units and jobs, CIIS tracks the square footage of new commercial real estate space, the number of individuals provided with credit counseling and homebuyer education, and the amount of additional investment CDFIs are able to make by leveraging their Fund awards. CIIS does not attempt to track qualitative benefits or more complicated quantitative benefits (such as the amount of money a household saves when the interest rate on its car loan goes down after the heads of household have repaired their credit history). Capturing these benefits is better left to in-depth research. CIIS data might support such research, but would not substitute for more appropriate research methods such as interviews and case studies.*

▶ **In FY 2003, CDFI financing helped to create or maintain nearly 8,000 jobs, develop or rehabilitate 40,000 housing units, and provide mortgage financing to more than 5,000 first-time homeowners.**

Among the benefits CDFIs bring to the communities they serve is financing for businesses and business development. By assisting businesses, many of them very small establishments, CDFIs help maintain and create jobs in distressed areas across the country. Businesses financed by CDFIs created or maintained nearly 8,000 jobs in FY 2003.

CDFIs also lend and invest in housing developers. These developers built or rehabilitated nearly 40,000 housing units, of which nearly 90% were affordable to low- and moderate-income families. CDFIs provided mortgages to more than 3,000 first-time homebuyers.

Saul Manriquez (right), owner of Carniceria La Especia, a grocery and meat market in Albuquerque, New Mexico with lender Greg Henderson (left) of ACCION-New Mexico, a CDFI providing micro loans to hundreds of New Mexico's entrepreneurs.

Finally, CDFIs finance commercial real estate development in economically distressed neighborhoods. These developments may include some rental or for-sale housing units in mixed-use facilities. They may also include community facilities such as charter schools, health clinics, elder care and childcare centers. The 30 CDFIs that provided data on the size of these developments reported that their financing helped to build or rehabilitate nearly 4 million square feet of real estate. These data are presented in Table 10-1.

Table 10-1: Community Development Benefits of CDFIs, FY 2003

	CDFIs	Benefits	Average Benefit Per CDFI
Jobs Created or Maintained by Businesses in CDFI Portfolio	94	7,878 jobs	84 jobs
Housing Units Developed or Rehabilitated	85	39,769 units	468 units
Affordable Housing Units Developed or Rehabilitated	78	34,611 units	444 units
Financing for First Time Homebuyers	53	3,093 homebuyers	58 homebuyers
Projected Square Feet of *Commercial Real Estate* Property Developed	30	3,681,845 square feet	147,274 square feet

 CDFIs provided *development services* to more than 50,000 people and organizations in FY 2003.

All CDFIs are required by definition to provide *development services*. *Development services* include technical assistance, training and financial counseling activities that assist potential and actual borrowers and investees to utilize the financial products of the CDFI. CDFIs provide many different types of *development services* to individuals, businesses, and non-profit organizations. A summary of *development services* provided by CDFIs in FY 2003 is shown in Table 10-2.

Table 10-2: Development Services Provided, FY 2003

	CDFIs	CDFIs That Offer Service	
	Number	Number	Percent
AFFORDABLE HOUSING SERVICES			
Homeownership Counseling	223	92	41.3%
Housing Technical Assistance	221	90	40.7%
ECONOMIC DEVELOPMENT SERVICES			
Business Technical Assistance	221	139	62.9%
Real Estate Technical Assistance	221	62	28.1%
CONSUMER FINANCIAL SERVICES			
Credit Counseling	221	96	43.4%
Financial Education	222	114	51.4%
OTHER SERVICES	216	86	39.8%

As the first column of Table 10-2 shows, nearly all of the 223 CIIS respondents replied to each question regarding the provision of *development services*. One sign of the importance of business formation and

development to CDFIs is the fact that nearly two-thirds (62.9%) of all CDFIs provided *business technical assistance*. Over half (51.4%) of CDFIs provided basic *financial education*. Credit counseling, *home-ownership counseling*, and *housing technical assistance* are each offered by about four out of 10 CDFIs. Additionally, over a quarter (28.1%) of all CDFIs provided *real estate technical assistance*. Finally, nearly 40% reported providing other types of *development services*, such as childcare facility design, assistance in obtaining government contracts, and technical training for wastewater systems.

Not only did a relatively large proportion of CDFIs report providing *development services* in FY 2003, the numbers of beneficiaries is also substantial. As summarized in Table 10-3, tens of thousands of individuals, businesses and non-profit organizations benefited from the three broad categories of technical assistance: *affordable housing*, economic development, and consumer financial services. Especially striking is the large number of clients who received consumer financial services and *affordable housing* development services, nearly 60,000 and more than 55,000, respectively. *Economic development* services were provided to just over 26,000 clients.

Table 10-3: Development Services Clients, FY 2003

	CDFIs	Total Clients Served	Average Clients per CDFI
Affordable Housing	117	55,211	472
Economic Development	140	26,418	189
Consumer Financial Services	93	59,469	639
Other Services	52	51,199	985

Recalling that CDFIs are quite modest financial institutions that average just 14.7 FTEs, the number of individuals receiving these development services is striking, ranging from 189 to 985 per CDFI depending on the type of service. With a minimum of resources, then, CDFIs reach many clients with technical assistance and training across many topics.

 CDFIs provide residents of distressed communities with access to basic *financial services* such as Automated Teller Machines (ATMs) and targeted services such as alternatives to predatory loans.

Depository CDFIs provide a range of *financial services* to residents of economically distressed communities. Table 10-4 summarizes some of these important services. All 36 banks and credit unions in the sample responded to each question. Services are grouped into two sets: general services and targeted services. General services tend to be available at most traditional financial institutions. Targeted services are those intended to serve low-income, immigrant, and/or "unbanked" populations. Targeted services include, among others, *Electronic Transfer Accounts (ETAs)*, which are the bank accounts required by the Federal government for all recipients of federal transfer payments such as Temporary Assistance to Needy Families (TANF) and veterans benefits. Targeted services also include *First Accounts*, a fairly new account established expressly for individuals who have never before had a bank account.

Table 10-4: Financial Services Provided by Depository CDFIs, FY 2003

	Percent of Depository CDFIs Providing Service
GENERAL SERVICES	
ATM Access	69.4%
Check Cashing for Customers/Members	83.3%
Direct Deposit	100.0%
Money Orders	77.8%
On-line Banking	33.3%
Youth or School Saving Programs	66.7%
TARGETED SERVICES	
Accept *Matricula Consular, ITIN,* or Other Form of Alternative Identification for Opening an Account	55.6%
Alternate to *Payday Loan*	52.8%
Bill Payment	30.6%
Electronic Transfer Accounts (ETAs)	69.4%
First Accounts	50.0%
Health and/or Life Insurance	38.9%
Non-Customer/Non-Member Cash Checking	38.9%
Remittance Programs	33.3%
Other Targeted Services	30.6%

n = 36

While the majority of CDFI depositories provide ATM access, check cashing, direct deposit, and money orders, it is noteworthy that nearly one-third does not offer ATM access and more than 15% do not offer check cashing services. Only one-third offers online banking. Those that do not offer these services include both banks and credit unions.

Access to targeted services is particularly important for the communities CDFIs serve. By offering these services, banks and credit unions provide a lower-priced alternative to the unregulated and typically high-priced check cashing, pawn shop and *payday loan* establishments that cater to low-income and immigrant populations. For example, check cashers typically offer payday loans. *Payday loans* are short-term loans secured by an individual's paycheck and used to meet short-term financial needs between paychecks. It is not unusual for check cashers to charge 15% interest per two-week period, the equivalent of 400% per year.[1] Over half (52.8%) of the CDFIs in our sample responded that they indeed offer a loan product that is an alternative to the high-priced *payday loan* available from local check cashers.

---

[1] Carr, James H. and Shuetz, Jenny: Financial Services in Distressed Communities: Framing the Issue, Finding Solutions, Fannie Mae Foundation 2001.

One reason millions of individuals are "unbanked" in the United States is the lack of appropriate iden-tification papers. Immigrants with an irregular immigration or work status may not be able to legally acquire a social security card, driver's license, or other forms of identification widely required by financial institutions to open an account. There are now, however, two alternative forms of identification available to individuals that cannot acquire conventional forms of identification. These are the *Matricula Consular* and the *Individual Taxpayer Identification Number (ITIN)*. The *Matricula Consular* is an identification card issued by Mexican consulates in the United States to Mexican nationals who have no other form of accepted identification. Over the past few years, many state and local governments as well as many financial institutions have begun accepting the *Matricula Consular* as a valid form of identification. *ITINs* are issued by the Internal Revenue Service (IRS) to foreign individuals who are required to have a U.S. taxpayer identification number. The *ITIN* is a nine digit number that resembles the social security number. More than half (55.6%) of the CDFIs responding accept the *Matricula Consular* or the *ITIN*.

Like traditional financial institutions, depository CDFIs offer a range of checking and savings accounts, including individual retirement accounts (IRAs) and certificates of deposit (CDs). As shown in Table 10-5, the eight bank CDFIs hold $291 million in just over 69,000 accounts, for an average of $4,200 per account. The 28 credit union CDFIs hold $246 million in two million accounts, for an average of $123 per account. The relatively low average balances reflect the low income levels of the typical CDFI client and, in particular, credit union clients.

Table 10-5: Types of Accounts Provided by Regulated CDFIs, FY 2003

	CDFIs	Total Account Balance	Number of Accounts	Average Balance Per Account
All Bank Accounts	8	$290,750,703	69,323	$4,193
All Credit Union Accounts	28	$261,443,302	2,001,796	$130
Individual Development Accounts (IDAs)	41	$2,047,012	38,723	$53
New Accounts Opened (Banks & Credit Unions)	28	NA	27,862	NA
New Accounts Opened by Previously "Unbanked" (Banks & Credit Unions)	15	NA	6,557	NA

CDFIs are instrumental in helping many individuals establish *Individual Development Accounts (IDAs)*. An *IDA* is a special type of savings account intended to help low-income individuals build wealth. For every dollar an individual deposits in an IDA, that amount is matched at least one-to-one by government, philanthropic or other sources. The savings in an *IDA* can only be used for purchasing a home, paying for education, starting or expanding a business, or covering job training expenses. Additionally, partici-pants are required to attend financial literacy classes. Together, these factors allow an individual to more rapidly accumulate wealth. Forty-one CDFIs, including 25 unregulated CDFIs in partnership with regulated CDFIs, provide their clients the opportunity to open an *IDA*. In FY 2003, these CDFIs were providing nearly 39,000 *IDA* accounts, or an average of 950 *IDAs* per CDFI. These are very modest accounts (averaging $53 per account) not including the matching funds. Nonetheless, the combined total value of these accounts was $2 million.

Not all banks and credit unions reported how many accounts they open each year. In FY 2003, 28 banks and credit unions provided these data and reported that they had opened nearly 28,000 new accounts. Just about half of these CDFIs track how many of their new accounts are opened to the "unbanked". These 15 banks and credit unions opened more than 6,500 accounts for "unbanked" individuals, representing 33.4% of the 19,344 of the new accounts these 15 institutions opened in FY 2003.

 CDFI awardees leverage each appropriated Financial Assistance award dollar with $19.63 in private and non-CDFI Fund dollars.

CDFIs not only invest their Fund awards, they use these awards to leverage additional private and non-CDFI Fund capital to support their community development finance activities. CDFIs are very efficient at leveraging and do it in three ways.

First, they leverage one dollar of non-federal funds for every dollar of Financial Assistance (FA) they receive from the Fund. This leverage meets the Fund's one-to-one matching requirement for FA awards.

Second, CDFIs leverage their net assets (or equity) to maximize the size of their primary working asset, their lending and investing capital. They leverage their net assets by borrowing against them. The Fund estimates debt leverage based on CDFIs' historical debt to net assets ratio and assumes that this ratio remains constant in the future.

Third, CDFIs leverage other funds at the project level. Many of the loans CDFIs make finance a portion of a project's total cost. For example, a real estate construction project typically has multiple sources of debt and equity financing to cover the cost of the entire project. These other sources may include banks, local or state governments, private investors and the borrower's equity. Project leverage is the amount of non-CDFI awardee dollars that go into the projects the awardee finances.

In the purest form, leverage means using a dollar to obtain more dollars. There is a cause and effect relationship: if the first dollar was not available, the additional dollars would not become available. When calculating the leverage of Fund awards, the Fund does not assume this cause and effect relationship, the reason being that it is very difficult to verify. For example, matching funds may or may not be a direct result of the CDFI getting a Fund award. Even if a private donor sent a CDFI a "conditional approval letter" stating that a donation is approved contingent upon the CDFI receiving a Fund award, it is not possible to definitively prove that the donor would not have made the even if the Fund did not provide the full award amount. Likewise, at the project level, it is not always possible to verify that the

CDFI's financing in a project led to the participation of other lenders and investors. For example, a CDFI provides subordinate financing in a deal. This lowers the risk of other lenders' senior position loans. However, absent interviews with the other lenders and a careful analysis of the history of the deal, one cannot conclude that the senior loans would not have been made if the CDFI had not provided the subordinate financing. For both matching funds and project level leverage, the Fund's methodology may therefore overestimate actual leverage.

On the other hand, the Fund may underestimate debt leverage. If a CDFI receives a Fund grant or equity investment in the final months of its fiscal year, it may not be able to raise additional debt against these net assets before the end of the fiscal year. In this case, the debt leverage figure will be underestimated: several months into the new fiscal year, it could jump significantly if the CDFI secured new debt. The underestimation may be relatively large depending on the amount of the Fund award.

 Leverage Calculations

The following table shows the three levels of leverage and is based on a sample of 23 CDFIs that received FA award disbursements in FY 2003 and provided sufficient data to calculate project leverage.

Table 10-6: Leverage Calculation, FY 2003

	Amount
REQUIRED MATCHING FUNDS	
Dollars Available to be Leveraged (total FA disbursements)	$17,317,901
= Matching Funds Leveraged ($1:$1)	$17,317,901
DEBT LEVERAGE	
Grant and Equity portion of FA disbursements	$14,542,901
+ Corresponding Matching Funds	$14,542,901
= Total Dollars Available to be Leveraged	$29,085,802
x Average (Liabilities / Net Assets) Ratio	1.41
= Debt Leveraged	$41,064,415
PROJECT LEVERAGE	
Dollars Available to be Leveraged (total FA disbursements + matching funds + debt leveraged)	$75,700,217
x Average [(Total Project Cost - Awardee Project Financing) / Awardee Project Financing]	3.27
= Project Leverage	$247,549,979
TOTAL LEVERAGE	
Total Dollars Leveraged (Matching Fund Leveraged + Debt Leveraged + Project Leverage)	$305,932,294
Leverage Ratio (Total Dollars Leveraged / Dollars Available to be Leveraged)	19.63

Project leverage ratios vary by loan purpose, with real estate loans tending to have higher leverage. As shown in Table 10-7, median project level leverage ratios are highest for multi-family rehabilitation (8.53:1) and construction (5.35:1), and lowest for business loans (.6:1 for fixed asset and .81:1 for working). These findings are consistent with what we know about these types of financing deals. Real estate deals tend to be large and complex, with multiple sources of private and public funding combining to finance the full cost.

Business deals tend to be smaller and simpler, with far fewer financing source. In fact, 29% of the CDFIs reporting project leverage data for fixed asset loans and 22% of CDFIs reporting project leverage data for working capital loans were the sole source of financing for the deals they supported.

Table 10-7: Project Level Leverage Ratios by Loan/ Investment Purpose, FY 2003

	n	Mean	Median	Minimum	Maximum
Business – Fixed Asset	38	1.90	0.60	0.00	12.91
Business – Working Capital	45	1.92	0.81	0.00	15.67
Home Purchase	17	2.90	0.84	0.00	15.01
Commercial Real Estate Construction	14	5.79	2.44	0.00	20.06
Commercial Real Estate Rehabilitation	15	2.06	1.53	0.16	9.00
Multi Family Housing Real Estate Construction	19	16.97	5.35	0.00	79.00
Single-Family Housing Real Estate Construction	23	9.36	2.25	0.00	46.49
Single-Family Housing Real Estate Rehabilitation	9	8.22	2.38	0.19	48.07
Other	22	3.86	0.82	0.00	49.23
Total	87	7.26[2]	2.14	0.00	115.86

---

[2] The mean total project leverage (7.26) does not match the average used in the leverage calculation (3.27) because only 23 of the 87 CDFIs included in Table 10-7 received award disbursements in FY 2003. The leverage calculation in Table 10-6 is based on these 23 CDFIs.

CDFI Survey

I. ORGANIZATIONAL INFORMATION
A. BASIC INFORMATION

Financial Institution Type

Organizational Structure

Street Address

City

State

Zip

Website Address (if available)

Telephone Number

Facsimile Number

1   Name of Person Responsible for Completing the Survey and, if
    Applicable, Transaction Level Data Submission

2   Telephone Number of Person Responsible
    (including Extension if applicable)

3   E-mail Address of Person Responsible

4   Date of Organization's Fiscal Year End

5   Year of Organization's Incorporation

6   Year Organization Began Financing Activities

B. ORGANIZATIONAL STRUCTURE / AFFILIATION

Ownership and Control by Minorities and Women

7   Is the Organization Minority Owned or Controlled?

8   Is the Organization Women Owned or Controlled?

9   Charter Number (Credit Union) or FDIC Certification Number (Bank or Thrift)

10 Is the Organization a "Faith-Based" Organization?

11 Did the Organization Finance or Provide Financial Services to any Religious Institution(s) or Faith-Based
    Organization(s) During the Current Reporting Period?

C. POPULATIONS AND GEOGRAPHY FINANCED DURING THE REPORTING PERIOD

12 Which of the Following Racial Populations Did the Organization Finance During the Reporting Period?

   * American Indian

   * Alaska Native

   * Asian

   * Black or African American

   * Native Hawaiian

   * Other Pacific Islander

   * White

   * Other

13 Which of the Following Hispanic Origin Populations Did the Organization Finance During the Reporting Period?

   * Hispanic or Latino

   * Not Hispanic or Latino

CDFI Survey

I. ORGANIZATIONAL INFORMATION

C. POPULATIONS AND GEOGRAPHY FINANCED DURING THE REPORTING PERIOD

14 Which of the Following Geographic Areas Did the Organization Provide Financing in During Reporting Period?

* Appalachia

* Colonias

* Hot Zones

* Lower Mississippi Delta

* Native American Areas

* Rural Areas

* Major Urban Area

* Minor Urban Area

15 Are 50% or More of the Customers or End Users American Indian, Alaska Native, or Native Hawaiian or Located in Native American Areas?

16 Native American Community Activities

Please Check Here to Confirm That the Table Below is Complete ☐

D. STAFF and CONSULTANTS : # OF FULL-TIME EQUIVALENTS (FTEs)

	Total Staff and Consultant Activity Breakout	Staff and Consultants
17	FTEs Dedicated to Lending/Investing	
18	FTEs Dedicated to Development Services	
19	FTEs Dedicated to Financial Services Other than Lending/Investing	
20	FTEs Dedicated to Administration and Other Activities	
21	Total FTEs	
22	Consultant/Contractor FTEs	

II. FINANCIAL POSITION

A. LENDING/INVESTING POOL

23 Investment Capital Table

Please Check Here to Confirm That the Table Below is Complete ☐

24 Investment Capital Summary Table

25 Off Balance Sheet Resources Committed to the Organization for Lending/Investing $

B. FINANCING COMMITMENTS THE ORGANIZATION HAS MADE TO ITS BORROWERS/INVESTEES

26 Financing Commitments to Borrowers/Investees at Reporting Period End. $

C. SUMMARY BALANCE SHEET INFORMATION AS OF THE REPORTING PERIOD END

27 Cash and Cash Equivalents Available for Operating Expenses $

28 Current Assets $

29 Loss Reserves

  a. Loan Loss Reserve -- Accrual $

  b. Loan Loss Reserve -- Cash $

  c. Depository Loss Reserves $

30 Total Assets $

31 Current Liabilities $

32 Total Liabilities $

33 Shareholders Equity, Net Assets, or Net Worth $

CDFI Survey

II. FINANCIAL POSITION	
D. SUMMARY INCOME AND EXPENSE STATEMENT INFORMATION	

34 Contributed Operating Revenue Table

Please Check Here to Confirm That the Table Below is Complete ☐

EARNED REVENUE

35 Interest Income Earned on Portfolio	$
36 Fee Income Earned from Lending Portfolio and Retail Financial Services	$
37 Interest Earned on Cash & Marketable Securities	$
38 Contract, Training, and Consulting Income	$
39 Other Earned Revenue	$
40 Total Earned Revenue	$
41 Total Operating Revenue (before gains/losses)	$

GAINS AND LOSSES (Realized/Unrealized)

42 Gains/Losses on Community Development Equity Investments	$
43 Gains/Losses - Other	$
44 Total Gains/Losses (Realized and Unrealized)	$
45 Total Operating Revenue (after gains/losses)	$
46 Total Non-Operating Revenue	$
47 Total Revenue	$

EXPENSES (Operating Expenses)

48 Interest Expense	$
49 Bad Debt Expense	$
50 Salaries and Benefits for Staff	$
51 Professional Fees	$
52 Other Operating Expenses	$
53 Total Pre-Tax Operating Expenses	$
54 Total Non-Operating Expenses	$
55 Total Expenses	$
56 Dividends Paid Out (For-Profit CDFIs and Credit Unions only)	$
57 Estimated Value of Additional Expenses	$

PRIOR YEAR REVENUE AND EXPENSES

58 Total Revenue in the Fiscal Year Prior to the Current Reporting Period	$
59 Total Revenue in the Fiscal Year Two Years Prior to the Current Reporting Period	$
60 Total Expenses in the Fiscal Year Prior to the Current Reporting Period	$
61 Total Expenses in the Fiscal Year Two Years Prior to the Current Reporting Period	$

CDFI Survey

III. FINANCING

A. FINANCING QUESTIONS FOR ORGANIZATIONS THAT ARE NOT SUBMITTING A TRANSACTION LEVEL REPORT

62 Will the Organization Submit a Transaction-Level Report for the Current Reporting Period?

63 Loans/Investments Closed Table

Please Check Here to Confirm That the Table Below is Complete ☐

	Amount ($)	Number
64 Amount of Loans/Investments Closed in Approved Target Market		

65 Portfolio Outstanding Table

Please Check Here to Confirm That the Table Below is Complete ☐

	Amount ($)	Number
66 90 Days or More Past Due		
67 Net Amount Charged Off ($)		

B. LOAN PURCHASES AND SALES

68 Loan Purchase Table

Please Check Here to Confirm That the Table Below is Complete ☐

Total Amount and Number from the Loan Purchase Table $

69 Sector Breakouts for All Loans Purchased During the Reporting Period

Sector Breakouts	Amount ($)	Number
Business Loans		
Commercial Real Estate Loans		
Mortgage Loans		
Other/Unknown Loans		
Totals		

70 Loans Sold Table

Please Check Here to Confirm That the Table Below is Complete ☐

Total Presale Book Value of Sale from the Loans Sold Table $

71 Sector Breakouts for Loans Sold During the Reporting Period

Sector Breakouts	Presale Book Value	Presale Book Value of Guaranteed Portion
Business Loans		
Commercial Real Estate Loans		
Mortgage Loans		
Other/Unknown Loans		
Totals		

C. LOAN GUARANTEES

	Amount ($)	Number
72 Loan Guarantees Closed		
73 Loan Guarantees Outstanding		

Page 4 of 18

CDFI Survey

IV. COMMUNITY DEVELOPMENT IMPACT QUESTIONS FOR ORGANIZATIONS THAT ARE NOT SUBMITTING A TRANSACTION LEVEL REPORT FOR THIS REPORTING PERIOD

		Number
74	Jobs in Portfolio Businesses at Reporting Period Start	
75	Jobs in Portfolio Businesses at Reporting Period End	
76	Projected Number of Housing Units Assisted	
77	Projected Number of Affordable Housing Units Assisted	
78	Number of First-Time Homebuyers	
79	Projected Capacity of Community Facilities Financed	
80	Projected Square Feet of Commercial Real Estate Property Developed	
81	Portfolio Companies That Have Decreased in Value in Past 12 Months	

82 Did the Organization Introduce Any New Products or Services During the Reporting Period?

V. DEVELOPMENT SERVICES

Types of Development Services Provided During the Reporting Period :

Affordable Housing

83 Housing Technical Assistance

84 Homeownership Counseling

Economic Development

85 Business Technical Assistance

86 Real Estate Technical Assistance

Community Development Financial Services (CDFS)

87 Credit Counseling

88 Financial Education

Other Services

89 Other Services (Not Included Above)

Number of Development Services Clients

CDFI Fund Programmatic Priority

90	**Affordable Housing - Development Services**	**Number of Clients**
	Total Clients	
	Hot Zone Clients Served	
	Target Market Clients Served	

91	**Economic Development - Development Services**	**Number of Clients**
	Total Clients	
	Hot Zone Clients Served	
	Target Market Clients Served	

92	**Financial Services - Development Services**	**Number of Clients**
	Total Clients	
	Hot Zone Clients Served	
	Target Market Clients Served	

CDFI Survey

V. DEVELOPMENT SERVICES

93

Other Services (Not Included Above)	Number of Clients
Total Clients	
Hot Zone Clients Served	
Target Market Clients Served	

94 Number of American Indians, Alaska Natives and Native Hawiians Served

VI. INDIVIDUAL DEVELOPMENT ACCOUNTS (IDAs)

95 Total Amount of All Open IDAs $

96 Total Number of Individual Development Accounts Open

97 IDA Withdrawal Purpose Table

Please Check Here to Confirm That the Table Below is Complete ☐

VII. DEPOSITORY CDFI OFFERINGS

A. DEPOSITORY ACCOUNT OFFERINGS - CREDIT UNION ACCOUNT OFFERINGS

		Amount ($)	Number
98	Regular Share Accounts		
99	Non-Member Share Deposits		
100	Share Draft Accounts		
101	Individual Retirement Accounts (IRAs)		
102	Share Certificate Accounts		

B. DEPOSITORY ACCOUNT OFFERINGS - BANK AND THRIFT ACCOUNT OFFERINGS

		Amount ($)	Number
103	Savings Accounts		
104	Checking Accounts		
105	Certificates of Deposit (CDs)		

C. DEPOSITORY ACCOUNT OFFERINGS - CREDIT UNIONS, BANKS AND THRIFTS

106	Bank or Thrift Customers OR Credit Union Members	

		Number
107	Number of New Accounts Opened	
108	Accounts Opened to the Unbanked	

D. FINANCIAL SERVICES OFFERINGS

109 ATM Access

110 Check Cashing for Customers/Members

111 Direct Deposit

112 Money Orders

113 On-line Banking

114 Youth or School Savings Programs

CDFI Survey

VII. DEPOSITORY CDFI OFFERINGS

D. FINANCIAL SERVICES OFFERINGS

Targeted Depository Financial Service Offerings

115	Accept Matricula Consular, ITIN, or Other Form of Alternative Identification for Opening an Account	
116	Alternate To Pay Day Loan	
117	Bill Payment	
118	Electronic Transfer Accounts	
119	First Accounts	
120	Health and/or Life Insurance	
121	Non-Customer/Non-Member Check Cashing	
122	Payroll Card or Other Stored Value Card	
123	Remittance Programs	
124	Other Targeted Services	
	Explain Other (If the Organization Provides Other Targeted Services, briefly explain these services.)	

VIII. DATA COLLECTION AND TRACKING SYSTEMS

125	Loan Portfolio Software	
	Other	
126	Borrower Characteristics Software	
	Other	
127	Community Development Impact Software	
	Other	

IX. CREDIT REPORTING AGENCIES USED

128	Credit Scores	
129	Reporting Agency	
	* Equifax	
	* Experian	
	* TransUnion	

X. SURVEY FEEDBACK

130	How Many Hours Did it Take to Complete the Survey?	
131	Comments	

XI. SUMMARY RATIOS

132	Average Net Revenue Ratio	
133	Net Asset Ratio	
134	Operating Liquidity Ratio	
135	Current Ratio	
136	Self-Sufficiency Ratio	

CDFI Survey

Certification Statement – CIIS Data Submission

Prior to the Fund accepting the data submitted by an organization, the user must certify, on behalf of the organization, to the following:

1   The person(s) entering the data and making these certifications has been authorized, by the organization for which the data is input, to enter the data and make the certifications.

2   The institution-level and transaction-level data to be submitted to the CDFI Fund through CIIS is true, accurate, and complete, and accurately represents the activities and/or performance of the organization for which data is input.

3   If the organization is a certified CDFI, the organization continues to meet the eligibility requirements for certification as a CDFI.

4   If the organization is a certified CDE, the organization continues to meet the eligibility requirements for certification as a CDE. The term "Organization" shall include the Allocatee and all of its subsidiary Allocatees, if applicable.

5   If the organization received a 2003 Native American Technical Assistance (NATA) or Native American CDFI Development (NACD) award, then 50 percent or more of the Awardee's or the Awardee's Partner's activities primarily serve Native American, Alaska Native and/or Native Hawaiian communities.

6   If the organization has received an award from the CDFI Fund, none of the proceeds of said award has been used to engage in the lobbying of the Federal Government or in litigation against the United States unless authorized under existing law.

7   As applicable, the organization maintains its existence as an Insured Credit Union, an Insured Depository Institution, or a Depository Institution Holding Company, as defined by the Appropriate Federal Banking Agency.

☐

Check Here if you Agree with the Above Statement

CDFI Survey

16. Native American Community Activities

Name of Native American Community

CDFI Survey

23 . Investment Capital Table

Source of Capital	Type of Capital	Amount	Interest Rate	Remaining Term (in months)

CDFI Survey

24 . Investment Capital Summary Table

Type of Capital	Amount	Percentage of Total Capital	Weighted Average Interest Rate of Debt	Weighted Average Term (months) for Debt

CDFI Survey

34. Contributed Operating Revenue Table

Type of Donor	Amount

CDFI Survey

63 . Loans/Investments Closed Table

Transaction Type	Purpose	Total Project Cost	$ Closed	# Closed

CDFI Survey

65 . Portfolio Outstanding Table

Transaction Type	Purpose	$ Outstanding	# Outstanding

CDFI Survey

68 . Loan Purchase Table

Purchase #	Purchase Date	Total $ Paid	Total # Loans	Presale Book Value

CDFI Survey

70 . Loans Sold Table

Buyer Organization Name	Total # Sold	Presale Book Value of Sale	Sale Proceeds

CDFI Survey

97 . IDA Withdrawal Purpose Table

Purpose	Number	Amount

CDFI Survey

CDFI Survey Notes

Question No.	User	Date	Note

The data analyzed for this report were collected during the Summer and Fall of 2004 through the Fund's Community Investment Impact System (CIIS). CIIS is the web-based data collection system that CDFIs use to submit their annual performance and compliance data to the Fund. This report analyzes the data CDFIs provided on their fiscal year 2003 activity, defined as the fiscal year ending in 2003.

CIIS includes two reports. The Institution Level Report covers the organization's financial activity and position, ownership characteristics, staffing levels and composition, development services, loans sales and loan purchases. For CDFIs that are not completing a Transaction Level Report, the Institution Level Report also covers financing activity, portfolio outstanding, and community outcomes. The Transaction Level Report includes details on each loan or investment a CDFI makes, including borrower and project addresses, borrower socio-economic characteristics, loan or investment terms, repayment status, and community development outcomes.

All CDFI Program and Native Initiatives awardees are required to complete an Institution Level Report per their Assistance Agreements with the Fund. At the time the data for this report was collected, CDFIs were not required to submit Transaction Level Reports, though six submitted a report voluntarily. The Transaction Level Report was a new reporting requirement that would not go into effect until CDFIs that received awards in FY 2003 began reporting for those awards (which in most cases was FY 2005).

CDFIs that are certified by the Fund, but have not received an award or do not have a current reporting requirement, may submit the Institution Level Report and Transaction Level Report voluntarily.

This report analyzes data from 223 Institution Level Reports and six Transaction Level Reports. For non-regulated CDFIs, only data collected through CIIS is included in the databases that are analyzed in this report. For banks and credit unions that reported into CIIS, their CIIS data is supplemented by the data they reported to the Federal Deposit Insurance Corporation (FDIC) or the National Credit Union Administration (NCUA), respectively.

The Fund requires CIIS users to respond to every applicable question in the Institution Level Report, though for some questions, "don't know" and/or "not applicable" are allowable responses. The Transaction Level Report includes mandatory, conditionally required, and optional questions. Transaction Level Reports are considered to be complete as long as all mandatory and applicable conditionally required questions are answered.

In this report, the number of observations for a particular analysis may be less than 223 for three reasons. First, the question may not be applicable for all CDFIs. For example, a business lender will not answer "housing units created" questions. Second, although the Fund encourages organizations to collect and report all of the requested data, some report *"don't know"* and leave optional questions blank. Third, for a small number of CDFIs, the Fund could not get definitive responses to all questions during the data cleansing process described below. For these CDFIs, if most of the issues were resolved during data cleansing, the Fund included that CDFI's data, except for the unresolved responses which are excluded from the analysis.

All information submitted via CIIS is subject to a data cleansing process. Cleansing involves confirming that the financial data submitted to CIIS are consistent with the organization's financial statements, assuring that the data provided are as complete as possible, and performing a set of logical checks to assure that all data within a report are consistent. A good example of a logical check is verifying that Total Investment Capital is equal to or greater than Gross Loans Receivable on an organization's balance sheet. If inconsistencies, apparent inaccuracies, or gaps are found in the data, the CDFI is contacted and asked to provide corrections. During the cleansing process and throughout the writing of this report, many CDFIs were contacted to clarify and in some cases correct their responses. Between these corrections and the restriction of this report to the cleansed dataset, there may be discrepancies between the results presented here and other Fund publications. For example, the preliminary community outcomes reported in the Fund's FY 2004 Annual Accountability Report were based on uncleansed CIIS data because cleansing was still in process at the time the report was being produced.

Once the data cleansing is completed, the data are imported into SPSS (Statistical Package for the Social Sciences), a program useful for mathematical and logical manipulation of data, storing data into databases, and performing statistical analysis. Using SPSS, frequencies (a distribution of the occurrence of values of a single variable or field) were performed on the age (in terms of the number of years of financing) and total assets of CDFIs. These distributions were used to categorize CDFIs into groups by their age and size of total assets. These categories were repeatedly used in the analysis throughout this report.

Appendix C.
EXPLANATION OF STATISTICAL TERMS USED IN THIS REPORT

CHI-SQUARE

Chi-square is a measure of the statistical significance of the relationship between two variables. The magnitude of chi-square varies with both the significance of the relationship and the number of cases involved in the analysis. Therefore, a probability statement, or p-value (such as $p = 0.03$), is always calculated with the chi-square. The p-value represents the probability (from 0 to 1) that the measure of chi-square is due to random variation alone. It is the p-value that allows the analyst to interpret the relationship as statistically significant or not. The conventions are typically to accept as significant $p < .05$ or (a more stringent test) $p < .001$.

F STATISTIC

The F statistic is a statistical measure of significance when there is more than two means to be tested. The chi-square statistic measures whether or not there is a statistically significant difference (whether or not these observations could have occurred by chance) between the means of two distributions. The F statistic performs the exact same function of accepting or rejecting the null hypothesis but for situations when there are more than one means to be tested. The F statistic is, in fact, a ratio between two or more chi-squares.

MEAN

The mean is the average score calculated by summing the values of a single variable (such as number of years old) and then dividing by the total number of cases. If there is especially large variance (the difference between the minimum and maximum value) in the observations, the mean might not be a particularly useful measure of central tendency. Indeed, for particularly skewed data (such as income information) the average is a rather poor measure of central tendency.

For example: The mean of these five values 1, 2, 4, 7, 135 = 149/ 5 = 29.8

The average, in this case, of these five values far exceeds all but one of the values, which demonstrates the possible distorted measure an average of a highly skewed set of values can represent.

MEDIAN

The median, along with the mean, is a statistical measure of central tendency of a single variable. Unlike the mean, which is the arithmetic center of the distribution of a variable, the median is the absolute mid point of the distribution. The median is that value where exactly one-half of the distribution is lower than this value and exactly one-half is higher than this value.

Using the same example above, the median is four, the middle value. One-half of the distribution is above this value; one-half is below. Very frequently, especially when the total variance of any single variable is high (viz., there is a very large difference between the minimum and maximum value), the median is much better estimate of a central tendency of a particular variable.

OUTLIER

Outliers are data that are either significantly larger or smaller than the rest of the data in a sample. Outliers skew the analysis by inflating or deflating the average. One way to determine if a datum is an outlier is by performing a simple descriptive statistical test that measures an observation's distance from the mean. This generates a z-score which is a standardized measure of the distance from the mean in terms of standard deviations. Under a normal distribution, about 97% of the observations fall within +2.00 to –2.00 standard deviations from the mean. Most statisticians advise disregarding for analysis observations that are more than 2.0 standard deviations and surely those that are 3.0 standard deviations from the mean. In this report, observations that are more than 2.0 standard deviations from the mean are identified as outliers.[1]

PEARSON'S SINGLE MOMENT CORRELATION COEFFICIENT (PEARSON'S R)

Pearson's r is a frequently used measure of correlation or association between two variables (such as height and weight among subjects in a health based experiment). Pearson's r varies only between +1.0 and –1.0, where +1.0 is a perfect positive correlation between two variables and –1.0 is a perfect negative association. Pearson's r, while a useful and simple measure of mathematical association between two variables, does not statistically control for other factors. Other kinds of analysis, such as regression, can help answer these more complex of questions. A rule of thumb when interpreting Pearson's r is that r = .75 or higher is a very strong association, r = .60 or higher is a strong association, r = .4 or higher is a moderate association, and r = .25 or more is a weak association.

---

[1]See, for instance, Herman J. Loether and Donald G. McTavish, *Descriptive and Inferential Statistics* (Boston: Allen and Bacon, 1993). Also, Ya-Iun Chou, *Statistical Analysis for Business and Economics* (New York: Elsevier, 1989), pp. 271-273.

Appendix D.
GLOSSARY

AFFORDABLE HOUSING: *Affordable housing* activities: (a) promote the supply of housing through the provision of acquisition, pre-development financing, construction, rehabilitation, permanent and other similar financing, and related development services, and/or (b) increase homeownership opportunities through the provision of first mortgage financing, subordinated mortgages (for home purchase and rehabilitation) and related development services. The housing must be the primary residence of a household or family that qualifies as low-income and that household or family must not pay more than 30 percent of their income on housing.

APPALACHIA: Appalachia is a 200,000-square-mile region that follows the spine of the Appalachian Mountains from southern New York to northern Mississippi. It includes all of West Virginia and parts of 12 other states: Alabama, Georgia, Kentucky, Maryland, Mississippi, New York, North Carolina, Ohio, Pennsylvania, South Carolina, Tennessee, and Virginia. A complete list of the Appalachian counties can be found on the Fund's website in the CDFI Investment Mapping FY 2005 CIIS Glossary System (CIMS). Users can access CIMS through the organization's myCDFIFund account at www.cdfifund.gov.

BUSINESS FIXED ASSET: A loan or investment that will be used to pay for any tangible property used in the operation of a business, but not expected to be consumed or converted into cash in the ordinary course of events. Commonly financed fixed assets include machinery and equipment, furniture and fixtures, and leasehold improvements.

BUSINESS WORKING CAPITAL: A loan or investment that will be used to cover any ongoing operating expenses of a business such as payroll, rent or utility expenses.

BUSINESS TECHNICAL ASSISTANCE: Assisting borrowers with business plan development including developing record keeping accounting systems, understanding critical expenses, applying for licenses or permits, accessing government and corporate procurement processes, and other related services.

COLONIAS: The Colonias include select counties in Arizona, California, New Mexico, and Texas. A complete list of the counties in the Colonias can be found on the Fund's website in the CDFI Investment Mapping System (CIMS). Users can access CIMS through the organization's myCDFIFund account at www.cdfifund.gov.

COMMERCIAL REAL ESTATE: Real property with intended commercial use, including retail, office, industrial, and community facilities.

COMMUNITY FACILITY: A facility in which health care, childcare, educational, cultural or social services are provided.

DEVELOPMENT SERVICES: A CDFI's activities that promote community development and are integral to the CDFI's provision of financial products. Such services prepare or assist current or potential borrowers or investees to utilize the financial products of the organization. Such services include, for example: financial or credit counseling to individuals for the purpose of facilitating home ownership, promoting self-employment, or enhancing consumer financial management skills; or technical assistance to borrowers or investees for the purpose of enhancing business planning, marketing, management, and financial management skills.

ECONOMIC DEVELOPMENT SERVICES: Services that support the development and retention of jobs and the start up and growth of businesses through (i) loans, equity investments and other similar financing to for-profit small businesses, microenterprises, and commercial real estate other than community facilities, (ii) related development services, and (iii) community organization support.

ELECTRONIC TRANSFER ACCOUNT (ETA): The U.S. Department of the Treasury designed the ETA as a low-cost account for individuals to receive their Federal payments electronically. Generally a nyone who receives (or represents someone who receives) one of these Federal Government payments is eligible to receive his or her monthly payments electronically through an ETA: Social Security, Supplemental Security Income (SSI), Veterans Benefits, Civil Service Wage Salary or Retirement Payments, Military Wage Salary or Retirement Payments, Railroad Retirement Board Payments, or DOL / Black Lung. For additional information go to http://www.eta- find.gov/Index.htm.

EQUITY EQUIVALENT INVESTMENT (EQ2): A loan that meets the following characteristics: (1) at the end of the initial term, the loan must have a definite rolling maturity date that is automatically extended on an annual basis if the borrower continues to be financially sound and carry out a community development mission; (2) periodic payments of interest and/principal may only be made out of the borrower's available cash flow after satisfying all other obligations; (3) failure to pay principal or interest (except at maturity) will not automatically result in a default of the loan agreement; (4) the loan must be subordinated to all other debt except for the equity-equivalent loans.

EQUITY-LIKE FEATURE: Equity-like features offer some upside potential over and above the return of principal and interest on the loan. The equity-like feature or kicker can be tied either to future revenues (royalties or participation agreement) or to equity (convertible debt or debt with warrants), or may include an interest rate that adjusts based on the borrower's performance.

FAITH-BASED ORGANIZATION: An organization whose founding (through capitalization or otherwise), governance, or membership is derived from a religious institution.

FINANCIAL EDUCATION: *Financial education* covers such topics as household budgeting, strategies for saving, benefits of saving, retirement accounts, and investments.

FINANCIAL SERVICES: Checking or savings accounts, check cashing, money orders, certified checks, automated teller machines, deposit-taking, safe deposit box services, and other similar services.

FINANCIAL STATEMENTS: Financial reports that reflect the financial condition of an organization at a specific point in time. Generally, such statements consist of balance sheets or statements of financial position; income and expense statements; statements of cash flows and, if applicable, auditors' opinion letters and any reports of findings (management letter), single audit reporting package (i.e., report on compliance with requirements applicable to each major program and on internal controls over compliance in accordance with OMB Circular A- 133), or any letters prepared by the auditor in compliance with OMB Circular A- 133.

FINANCING ENTITY: An entity whose predominant business activity is the provision, in arms-length transactions, of financial products, Development Services, and/or other similar financing. Such entity may be a: 1) depository institution holding company; 2) insured depository institution or state insured credit union; or 3) An organization which is deemed by the Fund to have such a predominant business activity as a result of analysis of its financial statements, organizing documents, and any other information required to be submitted as part of its application, use of personnel and total assets.
See 12 CFR § 1805.201(b)(2).

FIRST ACCOUNTS: A low-cost account and such other services designed to expand access to financial services for low- and moderate-income individuals, provided pursuant to grants made under the Consolidated Appropriations Act, 2001 (Public Law 106-554, 114 Stat. 2763, 2763A-126), and the Department of Transportation and Related Agencies Appropriations Act, 2001 (Public Law 106-346, 114 Stat. 1356, 1356A-44). For additional information go to www.treas.gov/firstaccounts/.

FULL TIME EQUIVALENTS (FTEs): An employee that works at least a 35-hour workweek. In calculating the number of full-time equivalents, part- time employees should be combined to full-time equivalents. For example, two part-time employees that each work 17.5 hours/week should be combined to count as one full-time equivalent.

GOVERNMENT SPONSORED ENTITY (GSE): A *government sponsored entity (GSEs)* is a privately held corporation with public purposes created by the U.S. Congress to reduce the cost of capital for certain borrowing sectors of the economy. Members of these sectors include students, farmers and homeowners, among others. GSEs include the Federal Home Loan Banks (FHL Banks), the Federal Home Loan Mortgage Corporation (Freddie Mac), and the Federal National Mortgage Association (Fannie Mae), among others.

HOMEOWNERSHIP COUNSELING: Assisting borrowers, who are new or existing homeowners, make informed decisions related to budgeting, selecting a home; types of mortgage insurance; home-owner tax benefits; equity build up; home maintenance, energy conservation, and foreclosure prevention.

HOUSING TECHNICAL ASSISTANCE: Assisting a housing developer to: Determine the financial feasibility of the housing property (such as cash flow projections, asset management, and identifying additional financing from public and private sources); conduct site reviews (such as environmental assessments, pre-condition surveys for rehabilitation, and evaluation of project location); and manage the construction project (such as ensuring construction standards, building codes and understanding restrictions).

INDIVIDUAL DEVELOPMENT ACCOUNT (IDA): IDAs are matched savings accounts, similar to 401(k)s that can be used by low-income households to purchase homes, seek post secondary education, capitalize small businesses, fund retirement accounts, or engage in other types of economic development activities.

ITIN (INDIVIDUAL TAXPAYER IDENTIFICATION NUMBER): An identification number issued by the IRS for tax paying purposes to individuals who do not have a social security number. For additional information refer to www.irs.gov or http://www.irs.gov/newsroom/article/0,,id=112728,00.html.

LOW-INCOME OWNED OR CONTROLLED: A business that is more than 50% owned or controlled by 1 or more Low-Income persons. If the business is a for-profit, refer to the owners. If a business is a non-profit, then if more than 50% of the Board of Directors are low-income, OR if the most senior manager (Executive Director, Chief Executive Officer, General Partner, or Managing Member) is low-income, then the non-profit is a low-income owned or controlled business.

LOWER MISSISSIPPI DELTA: A 240-county/parish area in an eight-state region comprising parts of Mississippi, Louisiana, Alabama, Arkansas, Tennessee, Kentucky, Missouri, and Illinois. A complete list of the counties in the Lower Mississippi Delta can be found on the Fund's website in the CDFI Investment Mapping System (CIMS). Users can access CIMS through the organization's myCDFIFund account at www.cdfifund.gov.

MAJOR URBAN AREA: A Metropolitan Statistical Area (MSA) with a population equal to or greater than 1 million, including both central city and surrounding suburbs

MATRICULA CONSULAR: An official identification card which is issued by the Mexican Government through its Consular Offices. The document only proves that the bearer is of Mexican nationality and is living outside of Mexico.

MINOR URBAN AREA: Metropolitan Statistical Area with population less than 1 million. Includes both central city and surrounding suburbs.

MINORITY OWNED OR CONTROLLED: A business that is more than 50% owned or controlled by one or more minorities. If the business is a for- profit concern, more than 50% of its owners must be minorities; if the business is a nonprofit concern, more than 50% of its board of directors must be minorities (or, its Chief Executive Officer, Executive Director, General Partner, or Managing Member must be minority).

NATIVE AMERICAN AREAS: Native American Areas and similar entities are defined as American Indian Reservations (federal and state); Off-Reservation Trust Lands; Oklahoma Tribal Statistical Areas; Alaska Native Regional Corporations or Village Statistical Areas; and Hawaiian Homelands.

PAYDAY LOAN: Short-term loans secured by individual's pay check, often at a high interest rate.

REAL ESTATE TECHNICAL ASSISTANCE: Assisting borrowers to determine financial feasibility of commercial property acquisition or expansion (such as cash flow projections asset management and identifying additional financing from public and private sources); site reviews (such as environmental assessments and evaluation of project location); and construction management (such as ensuring construction standards, building codes and understanding restrictions).

REMITTANCE PROGRAMS: Programs that allow customers to transfer or send funds to people in foreign countries. Often used by immigrants to provide financial support to their friends and family in their country of origin.

SECONDARY CAPITAL: Monies committed to an uninsured account with a low-income designated credit union for a minimum of five years. Funds in the secondary capital account (including both principal and interest earned) must be available to cover operating losses realized by such credit unions (i.e. losses that exceed its net available reserves and undivided earnings).

SECONDARY MARKET: A market in which an investor purchases a security from another investor rather than the issuer, subsequent to the original issuance in the primary market.

TARGET MARKET: For the CDFI Program, an Investment Area(s), a Low-Income Targeted Population or an Other Targeted Population.

WOMEN-OWNED OR CONTROLLED: A business that is more than 50% owned or controlled by 1 or more women. If the business is a for- profit concern, 50% or more of its owners must be women; if the business is a nonprofit concern, 50% or more of its board of directors must be women (or, its Chief Executive Officer or Executive Director, General Partner, or Managing Member must be a woman).

Note: This page left blank intentionally.

Appendix E.
COMPARISON OF THE CIIS FY 2003 RESPONDENTS AND THE CDFI DATA PROJECT FY 2003 RESPONDENTS

The CDFI Data Project (CDP)[1] is an industry collaborative that produces data about certified and non-certified CDFIs. The CDP partner organizations are the Aspen Institute, the Association for Enterprise Opportunity, the CDFI Coalition, CFED, the Community Development Venture Capital Alliance, Opportunity Finance Network (formerly National Community Capital Association), the National Community Investment Fund, and the National Federation of Community Development Credit Unions. The Fund was one of the founding partners in the CDP. In 2002, the Fund made the decision to begin collecting transaction level data from its CDFI Program awardees and New Markets Tax Credit Program allocatees, and subsequently separated from the CDP to focus on this new data collection effort. To a large extent, CIIS data points and definitions are consistent with the CDP.

The CDP conducted a data collection and analysis on the FY 2003 activities of 477 institutions. (See "Providing Capital, Building Communities, Creating Impact: Community Development Financial Institutions, FY 2003, Third Edition, a publication of the CDFI Data Project.) While the performance of institutions in the CDP sample is generally comparable to the performance of CDFIs in the CIIS sample, the Fund identified differences in the samples and discrepancies in some responses given by CDFIs that are in both samples.

 Summary comparison of the CIIS and CDP respondents

Nearly all (96%) of the CIIS respondents are Fund-certified CDFIs versus 61% of the CDP respondents. The financial institution type of the CIIS sample mirrors the universe of certified CDFIs, with the vast majority (80%) of CIIS respondents being loan funds. In the CDP sample, fewer than one-third of respondents are loan funds while more than half (56%) are credit unions. See Table E-1.

Table E-1: Financial Institution Type

	CIIS		CDP	
	n	% of Total	n	% of Total
Bank	8	4%	32	7%
Credit Union	28	13%	265	56%
Loan Fund	178	80%	159	33%
Venture Fund	9	4%	21	4%
Total	223	100%	477	100%

The composition of the portfolio outstanding of the CIIS data set is more heavily concentrated in housing (62%) while the CDP has less housing (44%) but significantly more consumer finance (23% versus 5%). See Table E-2.

---

[1] For more information on the CDFI Data Project, see http://www.opportunityfinance.net/industry/industry_sub2.aspx?id=236.

Table E-2: Value of Portfolio Outstanding by Sector

	CIIS	CDP
Business and Commercial Real Estate[2]	21%	28%
Housing	62%	44%
Consumer	5%	23%
Other	12%	5%
Total	100%	100%

The banks and credit unions in the CIIS sample tend to be smaller than those in the CDP sample, with CIIS banks having on average 60% of the assets of CDP banks and CIIS credit unions having on average 73% of the assets of CDP credit unions. The loan funds and venture funds in the CIIS sample have on average 7% to 10% more assets than those in the CDP data set. See Table E-3.

Table E-3: Average Assets (millions)

	CIIS	CDP	CIIS as a % of CDP
Bank	$ 106.4	$ 178.0	60%
Credit Union	$ 11.0	$ 15.1	73%
Loan Fund	$ 21.9	$ 20.4	107%
Venture Fund	$ 11.0	$ 10.0	110%
All CDFIs	$ 23.1	$ 27.6	84%

Tables E-4 through E-6 below provide summary financial and portfolio performance data for the CIIS and CDP samples. Appendix F provides additional portfolio quality analysis that can be used to compare the CIIS respondents to the CDP respondents.

Table E-4: Summary Statistics from the FY 2003 CIIS and CDP Analyses

	CIIS	CDP	CIIS as a % of CDP
n	223	477	47%
Total Assets (billions)	$ 5.2	$ 13.1	40%
Total Capital (billions)	$ 4.2	$ 12.3	34%
Portfolio Outstanding (billions)	$ 3.4	$ 8.4	40%
FY 2003 Originations (billions)	$ 1.7	$ 4.1	41%
Jobs Created (FTE)	8,000	NA	NA
Jobs Created or Maintained (FTE)	NA	32,000	NA
Affordable Housing Units Developed or Rehabilitated	35,000	45,000	78%

---

[2] "Business and Commercial Real Estate" includes business fixed asset and working capital, microenterprise, commercial real estate and community facilities financing. In CIIS, all of these fall into the Business and Commercial Real Estate categories. In the CDP, all of these fall into the Business, Microenterprise, and Community Facilities categories.

Table E-5: Portfolio at Risk (Combined Portfolio)

	CIIS	CDP
Banks	1.3%	1.6%
Credit Unions	2.0%	1.7%
Loan Funds	2.8%	3.5%
Venture Funds	3.3%	NA
All CDFIs Except Venture Funds	2.5%	NA

Table E-6: FY 2003 Net Loan Losses (Combined Portfolio)

	CIIS	CDP
Banks	0.4%	0.3%
Credit Unions	0.8%	0.8%
Loan Funds	0.6%	1.0%
Venture Funds	4.9%	NA
All CDFIs Except Venture Funds	0.6%	0.7%
All CDFIs	0.6%	NA

 Explanation of discrepancies in selected responses

The Fund identified 112 organizations that are included in both the FY 2003 CIIS and FY 2003 CDP samples.[3] These include four banks, 35 credit unions, 72 loan funds and one venture fund. Because there is only one venture fund, venture funds are not included in the comparison of responses.

The Fund selected five data points to compare across data sets. These are total assets, pre-tax operating expenses, earned revenue, net amount charged off, and value of originations. For loan funds, the Fund also compared loan loss reserves and portfolio at risk. For each data point, the Fund compared the responses each CDFI gave to CIIS and to the CDP.

In comparing the responses, the Fund analyzed the portion of responses that were exactly the same (zero variance), responses that were within 5% of each other, responses that were between 5% and 10% of each other, and responses that were more than 10% apart. The analysis was done by institution type. If all 72 loan funds provided the same total assets figure to CIIS and to the CDP, then 100% of the loan fund total assets responses would have zero variance.

For banks, the variance between CIIS and CDP responses was less than 10% across all cases, with one exception, this being the net amount charged off. For credit unions, total assets responses were always within 10% of each other; for all other variables, between 4% and 11% of responses varied more than

---

[3] Not all CDP respondents consented to the full release of their data, including their identity. Of those CDP respondents that did consent to the release of their identity, the Fund identified 112 that also responded to CIIS. The Fund recognizes that there are other organizations that responded to both; however, in the absence of the identities, the Fund could not compare the responses.

10% between the CDP and CIIS samples. The differences in responses for loan funds between the two samples are more striking. For five of the seven variables, 23% to 33% of the responses varied more than 10% and in some instances the variances exceeded 100%. See Table E-7.

Table E-7: Comparison of FY 2003 CIIS and CDP Responses to Selected Variables

Institution Type	Total Assets	Pre-Tax Operating Expenses	Earned Revenue	Net Amount Charged Off	Loans Originated	Loan Loss Reserves	Portfolio at Risk
BANKS							
n	4	4	4	4	4	0	0
% with no variance	100%	0%	25%	25%	100%	NA	NA
% with >0% and <=5% variance	0%	0%	0%	25%	0%	NA	NA
% with >5 and <=10% variance	0%	100%	75%	0%	0%	NA	NA
% with >10% variance	0%	0%	0%	50%	0%	NA	NA
Total	100%	100%	100%	100%	100%	NA	NA
CREDIT UNIONS							
n	35	35	28	33	31	0	0
% with no variance	97%	77%	64%	82%	94%	NA	NA
% with >0% and <=5% variance	0%	6%	29%	9%	0%	NA	NA
% with >5 and <=10% variance	3%	6%	4%	0%	0%	NA	NA
% with >10% variance	0%	11%	4%	9%	6%	NA	NA
Total	100%	100%	100%	100%	100%	NA	NA
LOAN FUNDS							
n	72	70	71	71	67	71	67
% with no variance	89%	71%	56%	72%	54%	61%	63%
% with >0% and <=5% variance	4%	14%	14%	4%	15%	6%	3%
% with >5 and <=10% variance	1%	3%	7%	0%	9%	3%	1%
% with >10% variance	6%	11%	23%	24%	22%	31%	33%
Total	100%	100%	100%	100%	100%	100%	100%

Two factors that could contribute to the discrepancies are differences in the way questions are worded in the CIIS and CDP data collection instruments, and variations in the respective data collectors' data cleansing protocols. However, the differences can not fully be explained without the Fund and the CDP contacting each CDFI individually. The Fund has had initial conversations with the CDP and plans to continue these discussions as well as engage the CDFIs to more fully understand the differences and find ways to minimize them in future data collections.

Appendix F.
PORTFOLIO QUALITY ANALYSIS,
COMBINED PORTFOLIOS

This appendix provides the portfolio quality analysis based on the combined portfolios of CDFIs in each group analyzed. It is in contrast to the portfolio quality analysis in Chapter IX which is based on the average portfolio for the CDFIs in each group. The combined portfolio analysis is the approach used by the CDFI Data Project.

 Portfolio at Risk

Table F-1 provides the combined portfolio at risk rates for the CIIS respondents by type and age of CDFI. The portfolio at risk of the combined portfolio of the respondent CDFIs is lower than the average portfolio at risk reported in Chapter IX: 2.48% versus 4.43%.

Table F-1: Combined Portfolio at Risk by Age and Type of CDFI, FY 2003[1]

	4 Years or Less	5 to 9 Years	10 to 17 Years	18 Years or More	All CDFIs
n	57	50	52	57	213[2]
Banks	*	*	*	1.10%	1.30%
Credit Unions	1.30%	*	3.01%	1.87%	2.03%
Loan Funds	2.03%	2.37%	3.67%	2.58%	2.77%
Venture Funds	1.14%	4.92%	*	*	3.25%
Total	1.87%	2.11%	3.26%	2.40%	2.48%

While overall this rate is modest, there are differences between CDFIs by type. The regulated CDFIs have smaller portfolio at risk rates than do the unregulated CDFIs. Banks and credit unions had combined portfolio at risk rates of only 1.30% and 2.03%, respectively, in comparison to 2.77% for loan funds and 3.45% for venture funds.

The portfolio at risk rates for the combined portfolios by age and size of CDFI are shown in Figure F-1. Clearly, examining the portfolios at risk by age and size of CDFIs differ somewhat. There is little variance in the PARs of CDFIs across age groups. Those CDFIs with the least experience in lending have a PAR rate hovering at or around 2.0%, while older CDFIs with more seasoned portfolios have PAR rate somewhat but not markedly higher. These same data examined by the size of CDFI, however, provides a different portrait. The smallest and largest CDFIs have low PARs (at or below 3.0%) while intermediate sized CDFIs, especially those with total assets up to $5 million dollars, had portfolios with a significantly higher amount of loans that where delinquent.

---

[1] An asterisk indicates that data has been suppressed due to insufficient observations.

[2] The data for 10 CDFIs are not included in the table. Seven of these did not provide portfolio data. The other 3 reported zero financing outstanding because one had not begun financing activities, another made no loans due to lack of funding, and another originated loans on its parent's books.

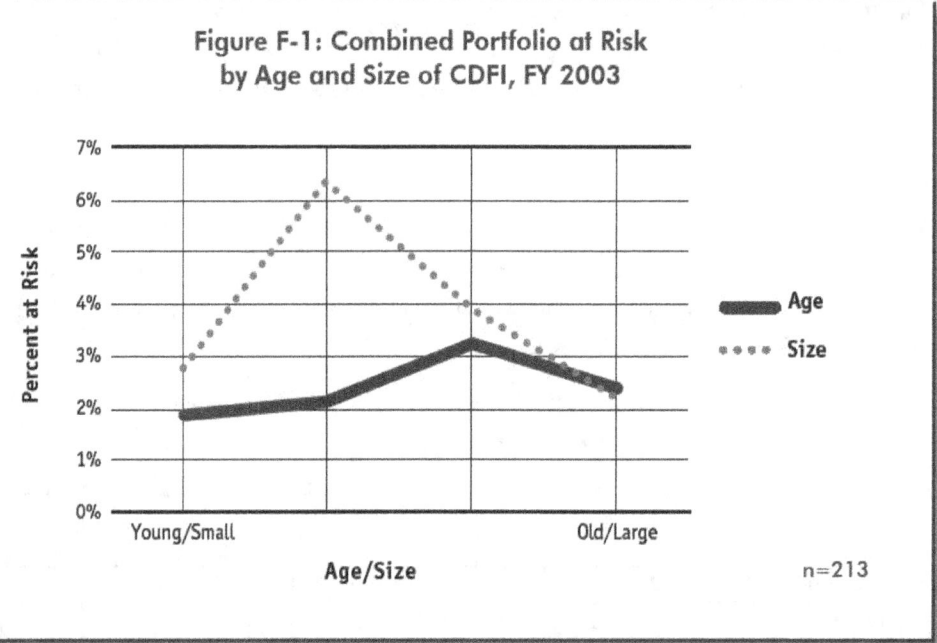

Figure F-1: Combined Portfolio at Risk
by Age and Size of CDFI, FY 2003

Loan Loss Ratio

The combined loss ratio for all CDFIs reporting in FY 2003 was only .65% with regulated CDFIs reporting only a .52% loss rate and the unregulated loan funds and venture funds having a somewhat higher rate of .69%. These loan loss rates by age and size of CDFI in FY 2003 are shown in Figure F-2. Looking at these loss rates by age first, we can see that with the exception of CDFIs with 10 to 17 years of lending experience, the loan loss rate is low and varies very little. For this one group of CDFIs, however, this rate is 2.25%, which while moderate is nonetheless over four times higher than any other age group of CDFI in FY 2003. Loan loss rates by size of CDFI provide a somewhat different picture. The smallest CDFIs show losses at 2.15% and those with total assets of up to $5 million have a slightly higher loan loss rate (2.75%). The final two groups of CDFIs, all with higher levels of total assets, have lower rate of losses of loans.

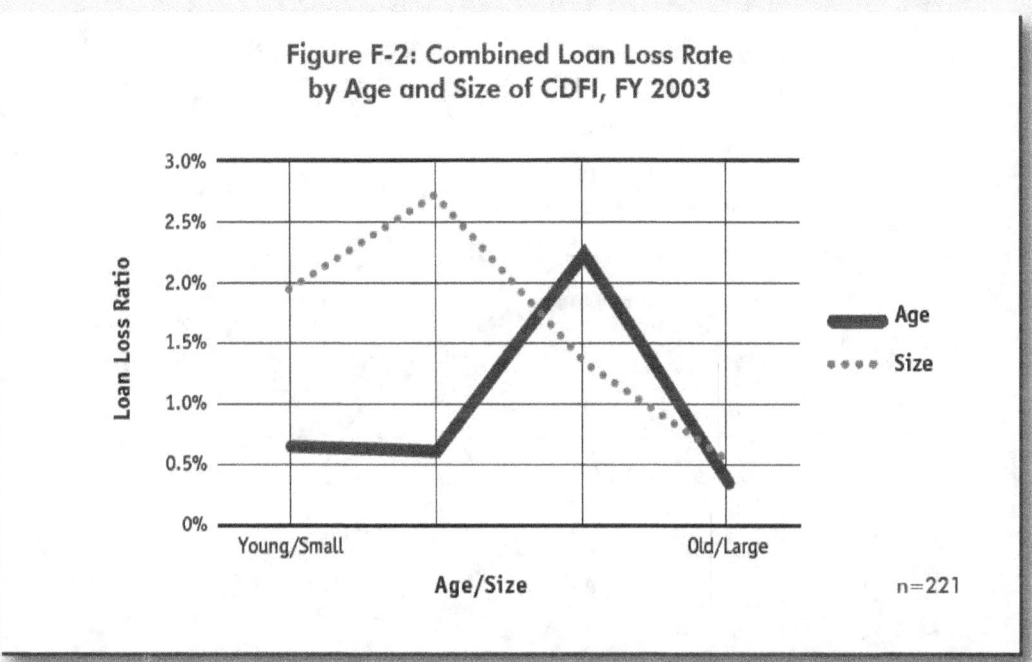

Figure F-2: Combined Loan Loss Rate by Age and Size of CDFI, FY 2003

 Loan Loss Reserve Ratio

The combined loan loss reserve ratio by age and size of CDFI is shown in Figure F-3. Clearly these loan loss reserve ratios of CDFIs in FY 2003 are quite similar whether we focus on the years of financing or total assets of CDFIs. Both plots are inversely curved: young and small CDFIs have relatively low loan loss reserves and initially as such institutions increase in size and increase their lending activities, such reserves increase. However, according to the findings presented in Figure F-3, CDFIs with 10 or more years financing experience and who accumulate $5 million or more of total assets decrease their relative levels of loss reserves.

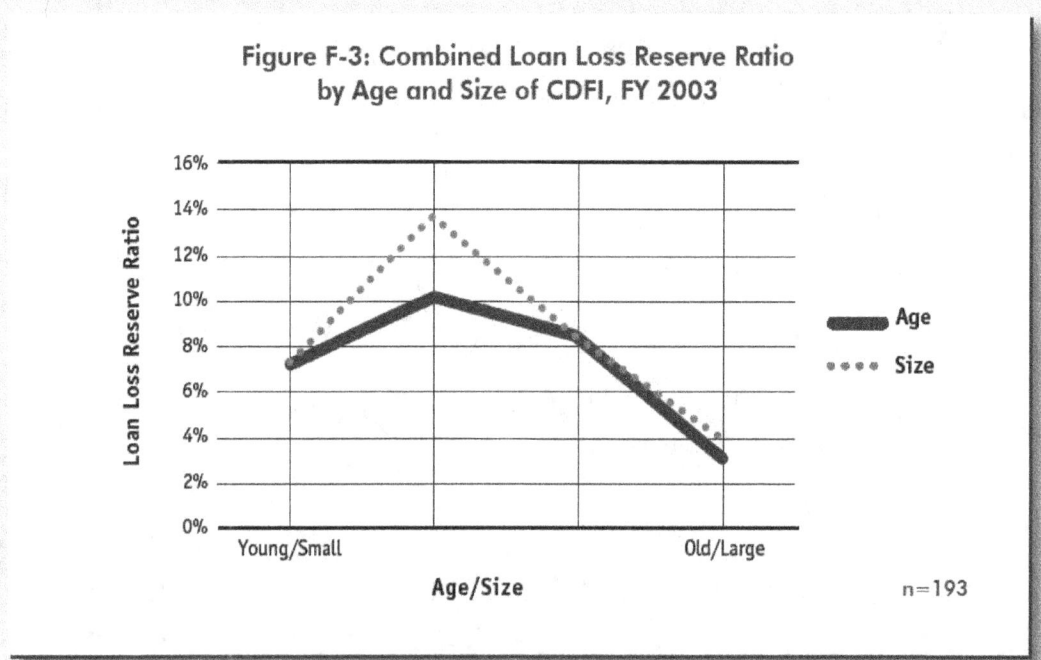

COMMUNITY DEVELOPMENT
FINANCIAL INSTITIONS FUND

UNITED STATES DEPARTMENT OF THE TREASURY

www.ingramcontent.com/pod-product-compliance
Lightning Source LLC
Chambersburg PA
CBHW080256290526
45790CB00005B/1829